Knowing It
When You See It

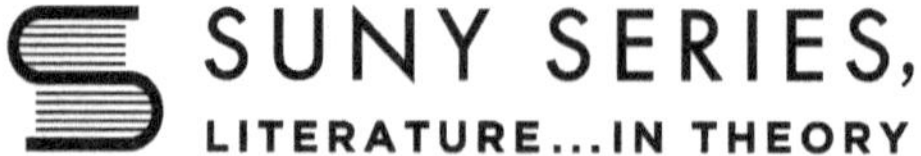
SUNY SERIES,
LITERATURE...IN THEORY

Knowing It When You See It

Henry James/Cinema

Patrick O'Donnell

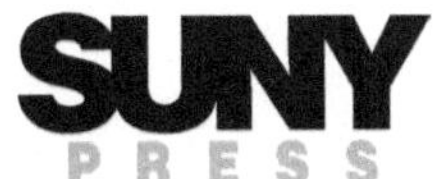

Cover credit: *Henry James*, © Michael Chaney; 8 in. × 10 in., oil on canvas board, 2015.

Published by State University of New York Press, Albany

Printed in the United States of America

For information, contact State University of New York Press, Albany, NY
www.sunypress.edu

Library of Congress Cataloging-in-Publication Data

Name: O'Donnell, Patrick, 1948– author.
Title: Knowing it when you see it : Henry James-cinema / Patrick O'Donnell.
Description: Albany : State University of New York Press, [2021] | Series: SUNY series, literature . . . in theory | Includes bibliographical references and index.
Identifiers: LCCN 2020022568 | ISBN 9781438482774 (hardcover : alk. paper) | ISBN 9781438482767 (pbk. : alk. paper) | ISBN 9781438482781 (ebook)
Subjects: LCSH: James, Henry, 1843–1916—Technique. | Motion pictures and literature. | Visual perception in literature.
Classification: LCC PS2127.T4 O36 2021 | DDC 813/.4—dc23
LC record available at https://lccn.loc.gov/2020022568

10 9 8 7 6 5 4 3 2 1

Contents

Illustrations

Acknowledgments

Many thanks to Scott Michaelsen, who urged this project to completion and cheered it on at every stage. Previous versions of chapters 1 through 4 were originally published in the *Henry James Review*, *The New Centennial Review*, and the *Arizona Quarterly*; my thanks to their publishers (Johns Hopkins University Press, Michigan State University Press, and University of Arizona Press, respectively) for permissions to reuse these materials. Thanks as well as to Ed Dryden and Lynda Zwinger, who allowed me to try out early drafts at the *Arizona Quarterly Symposium*; nearly forty years of conversations with Lynda about James and the example of her own work have been a constant source of inspiration. My great friend Justus Nieland in the Department of English at Michigan State University read the manuscript as it evolved, and provided invaluable commentary that has made the book immeasurably better than it would have been otherwise; his own capacious work on modern literature, film, and design has unfailingly contributed to my thinking and the stretch of my imagination. Memorable conversations bearing both near and far relation to the subject at hand with former colleagues in the Department of English at MSU, Scott Juengel and Jen Fay, as well as their stellar work, respectively, on the novel and film, have been essential. The faculty writing group at MSU (Ken Harrow, Josh Yumibe, Justus Nieland, Ellen McCallum, David Bering-Porter, Scott Michaelsen, Matt Handelmen, and Lily Woodruff) provided encouragement at a critical moment to go forward with this as a book project. Don Pease provided venues at Dartmouth for presentations of early versions of this work; like many, I have benefitted many times over the years from his intellectual example and his unfailing generosity. Special thanks to Josh Yumibe, who generously organized the frame enlargements to be found in the book, and whose knowledge of film and film materialities has been a constant source of illumination. I am especially grateful to Michael A. Chaney, artist, storyteller, and professor of English and African American Literature at Dartmouth for his permission to reprint his compelling portrait of Henry James on the cover. My thanks to Sheila Teahan for our many conversations over the years and for her own seminal work on James. I'm grateful to Coco Logan and Bob Moses, fellow gamers, good friends, and discussants extraordinaire of time, space, politics, Shakespeare, gender, and intellectual history. At SUNY Press, Rebecca Colesworthy's enthusiasm for the project has been essential to its completion and Jenn Bennett-Genthner's attention to production details is much appreciated. I finished this book during the fiftieth year of marriage to my wife, Diane, and nothing I have done would have been possible without her steadfastness and love. This one is for my daughter, Sara O'Donnell, my son-in-law, Ed Hill, and above all for my granddaughter, Luna Marie Hill, who is our sun and moon these days.

Vancouver, Washington
April 2020

Introduction

"The Business of Looking"

The "germ" for this consideration of Henry James and cinema comes from James's preface to *The Ambassadors*, his late novel of blindness and insight, where he describes a delightful "privilege" enjoyed by the "teller of tales" or the "handler of puppets." James—ever cognizant of the benefits and limitations that appear to descend upon the author like fate upon the chosen one, yet ever ambivalent about the power that he accords to himself as "teller" and "handler"—describes this privilege as coterminous with "the business of looking": "No privilege of the handler of puppets and teller of tales is more delightful, or has more of the suspense and the thrill of a game of difficulty breathlessly played, than just this business of looking for the unseen and the occult, in a scheme half-grasped, by the light or, so to speak, by the clinging scent, of the gauge already in hand."[1] The "business of looking" is applicable to any range of artistic disciplines, but the precise language of this passage is clearly cinematic. Visualizing the "unseen and the occult" in a narrative scheme "half grasped . . . by the light" could be said of the films of Alfred Hitchcock as easily as the novels of Henry James. Indeed, the initial connection I made when reading the preface to *The Ambassadors*, in an effort to better understand the relationship between James's narrative schemes and the visual imaginary of his late fiction, was the one that might exist between James and Hitchcock. If we regard the medium of film in Tom Gunning's terms as a "transparent" yet phantasmatic "filter of light, a caster of shadows, a weaver of phantoms. . . . [where] the act of seeing encounters a bizarre entity whose quasi-ethereal nature marks the limit (or contradiction) of visibility," we have a homologous approximation of how James regards the narrative medium as carrying out the business of looking for the unseen and the obscure in a scheme half-grasped by light.[2] A snapshot of the narrative scheme of the novel prefaced by James's description shows a protagonist, Lambert Strether, grasping at shadows cast amidst faint glimmers of epistemological illumination across three hundred pages of meticulous detail, concluding with certainty only about the limitations of vision and ephemeral hints as to all that might have been seen but has not.

The same set of connections between narrational and cinematic sensibilities might be made between any number of modern novelists and modern and contemporary filmmakers, especially since one of the primary assumptions of theoretical modernism is that its products are intensively intermedial and dependent upon visualization as the primary mode of representation occurring "within a larger history and economy of sensory perception that Walter Benjamin saw as the decisive battleground for the meaning and fate of modernity."[3] But, particularly in the late work and the prefaces to his novels that have constituted the basis for understanding his fictional strategies since their assemblage by R. P. Blackmur in 1934, James seems particularly prescient about the cinematic potential of his work inherent in his conceptualization of writing as an act of seeing. As Susan M. Griffin and Alan Nadel have surmised in an edited volume devoted to two men who "knew too much," Hitchcock and James: "James's sensibility was in many ways cinematic. He was profoundly concerned with the control of the gaze, with its powers and implications, long before there emerged a technology of animation to which the gaze would be central or a narrative medium based on that technology. He interrogated cinematic conventions for the most part before the medium of film existed . . . [James was] working, in other words, in a pure abstract laboratory of what might be called a cinematic imagination."[4]

In this book, I propose to explore how James's "cinematic imagination," as it is revealed in his late fiction and critical prefaces, is refracted in a series of modern/contemporary films that dwell on mutual concerns on how time and circumstance are to be rendered narratively and visually. James's critical prefaces were written near the end of his career for the New York Edition of his selected works, originally published in 1907–1909; coming in the wake of the late fictions that I consider here, from *What Maisie Knew* (1897) to *The Ambassadors* (1903), these prefaces serve as highly self-conscious commentaries on James's fictional architecture and methodology. Historically, the culminating years in which James regarded his writing of five decades as both an author and a critic were also significant years in the development of the cinematic arts: in 1907, the first ninety-minute feature film, *L'Enfant Prodigue*, was released by Gaumont, and the year saw the initiation of the wildly popular Broncho Billy western film series; in 1908, D. W. Griffith directed his first film, a short entitled *The Adventures of Dollie*, and a group of film producers joined together with Thomas Edison to form the Motion Picture Patents Company in order to corner the market on filmmaking in America; in 1909, there were 9,000 movie theaters in the United States, and the *New York Times* published its first film review.[5] In positioning the reflections of Henry James on his own novels in the late phase of his career alongside these signs of the emerging prominence of cinema in cultural life, I am not claiming that James was influenced directly by film, nor film by him. Although, as Susan M. Griffin relates, "James's fiction has provided a remarkable resource for filmmakers, inspiring over 100 film and television adaptations," and though he may have seen a handful of early, non-feature films (according to Griffin, "the seventy-minute film of the Corbett-Fitzsimmons fight word championship prizefight," "a short film about the Boer War in 1900," and perhaps a handful of others), in this book, I am not primarily focused on questions of adaptation or intermedial influence.[6] Rather, I wish to explore how James's late fiction and the critical prefaces of the New York Edition embody a culmination of ideas about vision, event, temporality, and perspective that had been percolating in his work from the beginning. These come to the fore during a time when a new medium is beginning to establish its own methodological and theoretical foundations within the "larger history and economy of sensory perception" serving as "the decisive battleground for the meaning and fate of modernity" that Hansen mentions. My idea is to focus on and explore a second culmination of James's twinned narrative and visual concerns in contemporary films that, as Frederic Jameson declares, provide ample evidence of an "increasing, tendential, all-pervasive visuality" spread across the history of modernity.[7] In so doing, I will pursue a set of correspondences between narrative architecture and cinematic architecture: James's late fiction reveals reflexive experiments in narrativity, perspective, the use of free indirect discourse, and the management of time roughly analogous to experiments in cinematic narration, set design, shot management, and editing in an array of modern and contemporary films that, through these experiments, manifest *their* reflexivity; both are invested in the relation between visible and invisible, and the totality or partiality of what can be seen.

In comparing several of James's late fictions to modern and contemporary films, my goal is to extend the arc initiated in this "moment" of modernity's inception from James's fiction to its manifestations in contemporary cinema. I deliberately avoid defining this arc as one that curves from "modernism" to "postmodernism" (or "post-postmodernism") because I do not wish to rehearse old and tired debates about the dividing lines and transitions between the two, or whether the latter exists as an epoch separable from modernism, or whether we have passed either or both by. Briefly, however, the relationship between James's fiction and modern/contemporary cinema can be viewed in the terms Fredric Jameson provides assessing the all-pervasiveness of visuality cited above in *Signatures of the Visible*. There, he claims to have previously misrepresented the dialectical and historical relationship between modernism and postmodernism in epochal terms. With the formal intervention that the development of cinema offers and a reassessment of the "asymmetry" it introduces into a dialectical understanding of the materiality of both the scriptural and the visual, Jameson claims that "modernism turn[s] out to be anything but an inverted realism, and postmodernism anything but a cancellation of modernity."[8] In other terms, film becomes the new entry into the history of forms and genres under capitalism that undermines any binary, epochal relationship between the "before" and "after" of modernism and postmodernism. Instead, the capacity of film to visualize reality in new ways transforms how we regard visuality in all mediums, particularly in the act of comparing two mediums—novel and film—which have established their preeminence as avatars of capitalized mass culture.

Of primary concern here, then, is how James's cinematic imagination and a thematics of visuality conveyed in his late fiction and prefaces offer parallels to modern/contemporary films engaging in experiments in the visualization of interiority, time, space, and event: these include Alfred Hitchcock's *Rear Window* (1954) and *The Birds* (1963), Michael Haneke's *Caché* (2005), Christopher Nolan's *Memento* (2000), Quentin Tarantino's *Kill Bill: Vol. 1* and *Vol. 2* (2003–2004), and Lars von Trier's *Melancholia* (2011). At first glance, such comparisons will seem odd and serendipitous, especially as I make no claims upon influence or genealogy. But in the readings to follow setting one of James's late fictions alongside one of these films, my purpose is to show how both raise comparative questions about knowing, seeing, and experiencing, and how these are registered in the chosen medium. One hesitates to use the word "meta" too loosely, but I believe it is fair to say that in his late phase and his prefaces, and at an inception point for modernism, James is practicing an art of metafiction (fiction about the making of fiction) that has resonance in the metacinematic films of Hitchcock, Haneke, Tarantino, Nolan, and von Trier, symptomatic of an age of "all-pervasive visuality." For James, a crucial aspect of his thinking about narration—the act of relating all of the details that go into a story including the interacting and (often) conflicting elements of plot, point of view, affect, geography, scene, dialogue, characterization, objects, "world"—is conceptualized in cinematic terms. Comparing James's "cinematic" thinking as revealed in his late novels, stories, and prefaces to the cinematic thinking as revealed in films by the directors I have named reveals the extent to which specific aspects and themes of a visual imaginary pervade modernism across time and media.

The central, oft-cited metaphor that James develops for his understanding of his own fictional architecture occurs in the preface to *The Portrait of a Lady* (1881), a novel indicative of James's increasing interest in the exploration of interiority and the resulting experiments of his late career in forging delicate, complex bonds between "reality" or "world" and an individual consciousness. In the preface to *Portrait*, James speaks of the "high price of the novel" as an entity so varied in its particulars that it continuously threatens to explode its own boundaries:

> Here we get exactly the high price of the novel as a literary form—its power not only, while preserving that form with closeness, to range through all the differences of the individual relation to its general subject-matter, all the varieties of outlook on life, of disposition to reflect and project, created by conditions that are never the same . . . but positively to appear more true to its character in proportion as it strains, or tends to burst, with a latent extravagance, its mold.
>
> The house of fiction has in short not one window, but a million—a number of possible windows not to be reckoned, rather; every one of which has been pierced, or is still pierceable, in its vast front, by the need of the individual vision and by the pressure of the individual will. These apertures, of dissimilar shape and size, hang so, all together, over the human scene that we might have expected of them a greater sameness of report than we find. They are but windows at the

> best, mere holes in a dead wall, disconnected, perched aloft; they are not hinged doors opening straight upon life. But they have this mark of their own that at each of them stands a figure with a pair of eyes, or at least with a field-glass, which forms, again and again, for observation, a unique instrument, insuring to the person making use of it an impression distinct from every other. He and his neighbors are watching the same show, but one seeing more where the other sees less, one seeing black where the other sees white, one seeing big where the other sees small, one seeing coarse where the other sees fine. And so on, and so on; there is fortunately no saying on what, for the particular pair of eyes, the window may not open; "fortunately" by reason, precisely, of this incalculability of range. The spreading field, the human scene, is the "choice of subject"; the pierced aperture, either broad or balconied or slit-like and low-browed, is the "literary form"; but they are, singly or together, as nothing without the posted presence of the watcher—without, in other words, the consciousness of the artist. Tell me what the artist is, and I will tell you of what he has been conscious.[9]

I cite this passage at considerable length because it will serve at several points in this book as a touchstone for the complexities and nuances of the narrative act conceived in visual and cinematic terms, though the latter was almost certainly not on James's radar as a descriptive word for his art.[10] James's aesthetic manifesto has several moving parts: the analogy of the "house of fiction"—seemingly, a kind of massive apartment house full of voyeuristic neighbors, telescopes and roaming eyes at the ready—conceptualizes fictional architecture, artistic consciousness, the singularity of observational frames, and the "human scene" as spectacle, all in one distended visual metaphor for which an exaggerated three-dimensional referent might be Gaudí's Casa Battló or Casa Mila in Barcelona.

At first glance, the analogy may appear to be panoptic. As Mark Seltzer suggests regarding acts of seeing in James's mid-career novel, *The Princess Casamassima* (1886), they can be viewed as instances of a "watchfulness" indicative of "Foucault's panoptic technology" with its "diffused, anonymous, and reciprocal—though always asymmetrical—operation."[11] Indeed, as I will suggest in the consideration of the prefaces and *What Maisie Knew* alongside Michael Haneke's *Caché* in chapter 3, James

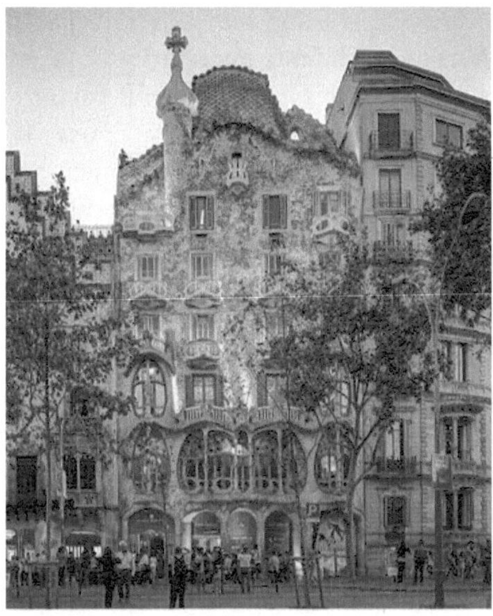

Figure I.1. Casa Battló, Passeig de Gràcia, Barcelona, Spain. Photograph by ChristianSchd. Wikimedia Commons.

reveals at several points in his novels and prefaces an anxiety about the impossibility of knowing and seeing "all," even while he recognizes that singularity—the particularities revealed by carefully framed and delimited vision—is his true game. Though he might at moments reveal a countervailing desire for access to the totality of the "human scene" available to a very privileged watcher at his window, James has too much invested in the more or less, the coarse or fine of the individual vision, which has its own privileged access to microscopic specificities of character, consciousness, and event.[12] Rather than being a figure for a rather baroque panopticon, James's "house of fiction" can be viewed—almost in Borgesian terms—as an infinite assemblage of singular, camera-eye perspectives. Behind each window is a discrete "watcher" whose access to "the human scene" occurs by means of the very shape and form of the aperture that, heretofore, had been a "mere [hole] in a dead wall," shaped and enlivened by "the need of the individual vision and the pressure of the individual will."

In the "house of fiction" analogy, James appears not especially interested in the totality of the scene, nor even whether all of these possible watchers collectively or collaboratively capture the whole of the "spreading field" before them. Neither does he seem interested in any consensus over what is being seen—in fact, just the opposite, he celebrates the diversity and infinite multiplicity of perspectives: "there is fortunately no saying on what, for the particular pair of eyes, the window may not open." From the perspective of his late career, twentieth-century hindsight, James is clearly rejecting the forms of literary omniscience and objectivism that pervaded the novel in the nineteenth century in favor of the "individual vision," though he retained throughout his work a love of the kinds of minute detail that one finds in Balzac or Flaubert.[13] The narrative techniques that he developed with subtlety and complexity as his fiction evolved included his well-known experiments with point of view, limited omniscience, free indirect discourse, and the location of a "central consciousness" or, as Sheila Teahan terms it, "reflective center" in a focal character such as Maisie in *What Maisie Knew* or Lambert Strether in *The Ambassadors*.[14] As I will explore in more detail in the readings to follow, if we view these strategies for the representation of consciousness through the lens provided in James's "house of fiction" analogy, the figures are strikingly cinematic. Each "watcher gazes" at the "scene" through an aperture that frames, shapes, and filters what is seen; each "pair of eyes" or "field glass" is instrumentally rendered as a technological formation that both witnesses and constructs what is seen; the activity in which all are engaged is both observational and voyeuristic, the latter, according to film theorists ranging from Sergei Eisenstein and André Bazin to Laura Mulvey and Slavoj Žižek, a primary component of film's materiality as well as its subject matter. James could not possibly have foreseen the current moment in which billions of watchers on the planet seem to be viewing reality through the camera eyes of their cell phones, and the very thought probably would have horrified him deeply, but the image of the "house of fiction" seems an eerie prognosticator of the ways in which "consciousness" is viewed as consonant with watching and seeing through an aperture, the very modus operandi of cinema from those involved in film's making.

Yet much as it may appear on superficial glance that James is attempting to democratize those acts of seeing and vision implicit in the role of authorship (it is all "as nothing without the posted presence of the watcher—without, in other words, the consciousness of the artist"), it is clear from the centralization of consciousness in his novels that some see "more" or have privileged perspectives, a position James would reserve for the greatest artists, including himself. Seeing more, in James, is seeing better, and, as I will discuss in the reading of *What Maisie Knew* in chapter

3, seeing "most" is the ultimate, unachievable goal since, as the "house of fiction" analogy suggests, the human scene "spreads" to infinity, and the number of apertures through which it can be viewed are "not to be reckoned." Herein lies a central paradox, for while the analogy seems to imply a boundless array of singular perspectives (each to their own cell phone), it also implies that there is a totality behind it all, *one* "human scene," *one* reality that is to be beheld, a "whole" that all of those holes in the wall pertain to. On the one hand, the singularity and privilege of authorial consciousness. On the other hand, a desire for an impossible total vision, a desire to somehow see everything incapsulated in those Jamesian stories that I will consider in detail here: a child who sees too much (*What Maisie Knew*); a woman who sees and knows much more than she should (the telegraph operator of "In the Cage," 1898), a man who wants to know everything about his own future, conceived as a horror show ("The Beast in the Jungle," 1903); and a man who knows too little in America and too much in Paris, leading him to view "life" as a process of discovering what one should have known all along (*The Ambassadors*).

As an artist, James feels an obligation to render visible everything that he sees precisely as *everything that could be seen* in his fictions, yet acknowledges at the same time that only through the singular, privileged perspective that frames and delimits what is seen and known can a "view" take shape at all. James makes clear that he recognizes the contradiction in the preface to *Roderick Hudson* (1875), where it causes him no little authorial anxiety. Writing from the perspective of an elderly, accomplished statesmen of the novel in the Preface, James recalls the anxieties he felt about launching his early novel upon "the blue southern sea" (his reflections are replete with nautical metaphors) and giving shape and form to the ocean of reality that surrounded him.[15] He speaks of "the ache of fear, that was to become so familiar, of becoming unduly tempted and led on by 'developments' "; he describes the challenges inherent in giving structure to the unbounded scene before him with its myriad possibilities; and he confesses to the "proportionate anxiety" involved in discerning certain relations between certain elements of the observed scene, which is the at the heart of artistic labor in offering "the complete expression of one's subject."[16] But where, James asks, "does a particular relation stop—giving way to some other not concerned in that expression?"[17]

This formalist concern is deepened a few sentences later in the Preface when James develops another metaphor for the work of the artist, that of an embroiderer or seamstress:

> Really, universally, relations stop nowhere, and the exquisite problem of the artist is eternally but to draw, by a geometry of his own, the circle within which they shall happily appear to do so. He is in the perpetual predicament that the continuity of things is the whole matter, for him, of comedy and tragedy; that this continuity is never, by the space of an instant or an inch, broken, and that, to do anything at all, he has at once intensely to consult and intensely to ignore it. All of which will perhaps pass but for a supersubtle way of pointing the plain moral that a young embroiderer of the canvas of life soon began to work in terror, fairly, of the vast expanse of that surface, of the boundless number of its distinct perforations for the needle, and of the tendency inherent in his many-colored flowers and figures to cover and consume as many as possible of the little holes. The development of the flower, of the figure, involved thus an immense counting of holes and a careful selection among them. That would have been, it seemed to him, a brave enough process, were it not the very nature of the holes so to invite, to solicit, to persuade, to practice positively a thousand lures and deceits.[18]

Like the depiction of "the house of fiction" in the preface to *The Portrait of Lady*, I will loop back to this image of "the canvas of life" at several points in this book as it incrementally informs the consideration of conceptions of totality and singularity in James's late fiction. In succeeding terms of "fear," "anxiety," and ultimately "terror," James thus formulates the quandary that confronts the artist invested in representing the totality of "the vast expanse of that surface"—"the canvas of life"—but who knows that he must resist the "thousand lures and deceits" of endless detail if he is focalize the embroidery of a singular flower or stitch the relations between a specific set of figures. While James attributes much of the affect attached to the question of how to deal with the totality of the whole and the particularities of "development" to youth in this portrait of the artist as a young man, he also makes it clear that the fear and anxiety involved in framing and stitching up reality into the specificities of chosen figures haunt his thinking about artistic work throughout his career. I will return to this complex analogy in chapter 1, where it sheds light on James's and Hitchcock's shared attraction to the lure of detail. But placed alongside the "house of fiction" analogy and as they play out in his novels and stories, the two prefaces reveal an array of epistemological and visual anxieties: the desire to know and see as much as possible, accompanied by the fear of knowing and seeing too much or too little; and the recognition that there is a kind of totality (a vast expanse, the human scene) to be examined, along with a recognition that there must be an achieved perspective for that totality to be visible. Both analogies figure acts of seeing and knowing in terms of holes, wholes, gaps, filters, and windows; the fenestrated perspectivism of the "house of fiction" exists alongside the pointillist embroidery of "the canvas of life." Both instantiate intensely visual metaphors, reflecting the author's anxious recognition that the totality of "life" or "scene" can be peered at through the severe limitations of the singular frame, the directed view, the many gaps in the weave of the canvas not filled amidst the embroidered few. For the works I will discuss in this book, this central conundrum informs both the production and content of James's fiction, as characters struggle to frame and reframe a constantly shifting "human scene," as narrators, peering around the corner, frame and reframe these struggles, and as James, the author, reflects on his constructions of the, paradoxically, singular totalities of his novels.[19]

The conundrum informs the intertwined histories of the modern novel and cinema as well. Two foundational theorists of the evolution of the modern novel and the development of cinema, György Lukács and André Bazin, respectively, frame questions about totality and medium in ways strikingly similar to that of James in his prefaces. In *The Theory of the Novel*, Lukács develops the concept of "totality" as present and immanent in the age of the epic, which could represent "life" as "contain[ing] within itself both the relative independence of every separate living being from any transcendent bond and the likewise relative inevitability and indispensability of such bonds."[20] From Lukács's historical perspective, the novel "is the epic of an age [that of modernity] in which the extensive totality of life is no longer directly given, in which the immanence and meaning of life has become a problem, yet which still thinks in terms of a totality."[21] For Lukács, as for James, the novel serves as a form of access to this totality (the human scene, the canvas of life) only indirectly, formalistically, via a manufactured perspective: "The epic gives form to a totality of life that is rounded from within; the novel seeks, by giving form, to uncover and construct the totality of life."[22] To be sure, James is much less nostalgic than Lukács for the kind of direct, "epic" access to the immanent totality of life, for he sees the novel much more clearly than Lukács in terms of its medium and materiality. The novel *is*, for James, a multi-windowed portal opening out onto modern life as we know it, a spreading, open-ended, even rhizomic assemblage of relations going everywhere to be culled by the discerning artist dedicated to providing singular, centralized perspectives that limn the whole as much by what they leave out as what they put in. Yet both Lukács and James identify in the history and form of the novel a problematic relationship between the genre and its modern status as a mediator of "life," conceived as a totality to which the novel has some kind of privileged access. Especially for James, this access—this portal to the whole—is both empowered and delimited by its materiality as a shaped lens or framed window opening out upon "life" and "scene."

In "The Myth of a Total Cinema," a chapter in the foundational *What is Cinema?*, André Bazin articulates a strikingly similar problematic operating with the emergence of film, the exemplar of mass media in the first half of the twentieth century. Bazin writes that the "idea" of cinema precedes the technology by which it came about.[23] In the minds of those avatars and inventors of what he terms "photographic cinema" and the technology that enabled "the automatic fixing of the image," there existed an idealization of the medium *avant la lettre*: "In their imaginations, they saw the cinema as a total and complete representation of reality; they saw in a trice the reconstruction of a perfect illusion of the outside world in sound, color and relief."[24] Bazin goes on to critique this myth at the origins of a genre and discipline that, in his view, is founded upon "the primacy of the image": "The guiding myth, then, inspiring the invention of cinema, is the accomplishment of that which dominated in a more or less vague fashion all the techniques of the mechanical reproduction of reality in the nineteenth century, from photography to the phonograph, namely an integral realism, a recreation of the world in its own image, an image unburdened by the freedom of interpretation of the artist or the irreversibility of time."[25] But interpretation and technological limitation, Bazin suggests, are part and parcel of the medium itself, despite any implicit desire to capture the whole of reality for the first time via a new technology that automates imagistic primacy. James's watchers at the window—those embodiments of "the consciousness of the artist" with their multiple angles of vision upon a scene—are necessary to a medium that only exists because of their presence. For Bazin, film cannot even begin to address its hopes for the inculcation of an "integral realism," the total "world in its own image," save through a cinematic apparatus wholly reliant upon interpretation and instrument (shots, camera angles, directors, actors, scene constructions, lighting schematics) for it to come about *as* film.

Two common elements emerge in the "meta" statements of James, Lukács, and Bazin about the status of mediums they consider in light of an implicit desire that they reflect, or fail to reflect, a totality variously referred to as "world," "scene," or "life." We might call these the "facts" of intermediality existing in the modern novel (for which James surely serves as source and avatar) and the modern genre of film from its inception.[26] The first is the "fact" of a reality composed of multiple perspectives. The novel for James, especially as it is characterized in his prefaces and exemplified in his late fiction, is focused on interlocking or conflicting perspectives and angles of vision, as well as the misunderstandings and affective imbalances that can occur as the result of characters exchanging perspectives in dialogue. A film, of course, considered in the broadest possible terms, is composed of a series of shots, angles of vision, and directed "scenes" that are edited together to produce a whole made up of parts rendered by the multiple, overlaid interpretations of the director, cinematographer, film editor, screenwriter, and others as to what should be seen and screened. The second, as this characterization of what is involved in the making of a film makes clear, is the "fact" of collaboration. On the one hand, while James—the "master" as he is often termed[27]—is the sole writer, director, and producer of his novels (as well as serving as set decorator, costume designer, and dialogue coach), the prefaces and the narrative strategies he increasingly deploys as he moves into his late phase clearly suggest that he views the making and content of his fiction in collaborative terms, both visually and narratologically. The novels and stories I shall discuss in this book work are assemblages of multiple perspectives, some privileged, some not, charting intersubjective relationships between consciousnesses matched and mismatched in terms of intelligence, scope and range of vision, wit, and ability to adapt to unstable social environments. The environment itself, in these fictions, whether one uses the term "human scene" or "mise-en-scène," is activated through directed angles of vision and the elaboration of perceptions arising from a series of finely detailed "consciousnesses" seeing, hearing, and absorbing through the senses the "world" around them. Like the cinematic auteurs that I will discuss here—Hitchcock, Nolan, Tarantino, Haneke, von Trier—each signing their collaborative work as masters through their recognizable directorial stamp, James clearly insists, among all those watchers at various windows, that his view is primary, yet the view itself, in its framing offers an anxious recognition that it is but a single portal opening onto an ungraspable, manifold totality only revealed through a collaboration of minds.

I will be pursuing the specific consequences of the complex set of connections between medium, artist, and world in considering how these occur in the work of a modernist "master" who thinks about writing in visual terms, and six modern/contemporary films that trouble these connections visually and narratively in ways comparable to James. The troubling traces an arc, between a moment when the novel, as Lukács suggests, was beginning to be anxious about its capacity to encompass a reality that was now accessible through other means (photography and film) and an era of cinematic primacy where film, in the hands of several auteur directors, engages with questions about *its* capacity to engage with reality through the limitations of the medium. Subtending this arc is the fantasy of a totality that has its secular foundations in late capitalism where "the concept of the market lies in its 'totalizing' structure . . . that is, in its capacity to afford a model of social totality."[28] How a novelist perched at the beginning of a new century thinks "narratively/visually" about his work as a form of mediation between consciousness and world, and how, comparatively, a handful of filmmakers riding the cinematic wave from mid-century on think "visually/narratively" about the same thing, yet differently, because the medium is different, comprises the connective tissue of this book.

Specifically, in chapter 1, I consider James's novella "In the Cage" alongside Hitchcock's *The Birds* as works invested in coming to terms with human subjectivity as an entity devoted to discerning the intentionality of a perceived totality toward the iconic singularity of the individual, and the intentionality of the individual toward the world. Both Hitchcock and James gravitate toward the "lure of detail" mentioned previously, and the protagonists of the two narratives represented in the film and the novella are confronted with a barrage of singularities comprising a whole (birds, codes, signals, messages) that they are compelled to comprehend in the form of an intention. The impossibility of doing so informs the dramatic tension of the novella and the film, and poses certain technical problems for both the novelist and the director: How, for Hitchcock, to visually represent the universality of the birds as an overwhelming catastrophe through specific events, locations, and entities that cannot possibly be made to flock together? How, for James, to represent the purchase on social and political knowledge save through a serendipitous array of messages that can only be partially decoded? For both, how is the social order to be viewed when it is recognized that it is made up of myriad details that do not add up to discernable purpose or intention? Both face in these highly reflexive works the question of what is to be done when, in effect, the camera can only infer the reality it visualizes, and the novel can only provide an angular purchase on the world it seeks to establish.

In chapter 2, a comparison of James's *What Maisie Knew* and Tarantino's *Kill Bill: Vol. 1* and *Vol. 2* provides an occasion for considering the ways in which one of the novelist's most complex and touching portrayals of the destruction of innocence can be read in light of the director's ultra-violent *bildungspiel*, where the central dramatic concern is the nature of a parent-child relationship when its narrativization takes place within a social order wholly given over to mortality. In her voice from the dead, William Faulkner's Addie Bundren states a pedagogical principle: "I could just remember how my father used to say that the reason for living was to get ready to stay dead a long time."[29] The same principle, with variations, is expounded in *What Maisie Knew* and *Kill Bill.* In James, childhood living is a series of merciless plunges into an adult world of sexual conspiracy and betrayal; Maisie is "nothing" in her own right save an epistemological reservoir for "improper" desire, and her imagined parent-murder in the closing scenes of the novel is but the logical outcome (as staying dead is for Addie) of living in the world constructed about her. In Tarantino, childhood living is but the initial stage in a mortal apprenticeship for a fully achieved "adulthood" that seems to inevitably involve daily hand-to-hand combat in the desire for revenge and the struggle for survival. James's mannerism is matched by Tarantino's naturalism in their mutual regard of time passing as the "material" of knowledge and experience. Narratologically and cinematically, both James and Tarantino foreground temporality in these stories of maturation at the intersection of content and medium. For James, it becomes a question of how the centralized consciousness of Maisie can come to know the unknown, and how much of the unknown is knowable. Tarantino, via the furious, hyperkinetic citations of the *Kill Bill* films, pressures the extent to which the cinematic medium visualizes its own phantasmatic nature and, as Murray Pomerance has defined it, the primary condition of its modernity—its temporariness, nothing but time passing while passing time.[30] Both novel and film, in this regard, approach the limits of their capacity to render worlds of their own making.

Total vision is the subject of chapter 3. Extending the discussion of *What Maisie Knew* to *The Wings of the Dove*, the prefaces to *Roderick Hudson* and *The Golden Bowl*, and Haneke's *Caché*, this chapter considers the fantasies constitutive of what Slavoj Žižek terms the "parallax view." This is a condition of post-Einsteinian modernity where the recognition that the materiality of the object can change in relation to the position of the observer produces "a reflexive twist by means of which I am myself included in the picture constituted by me . . . [a] redoubling of myself as standing both inside and outside [the] picture."[31] For James, this recognition is cultivated within the protagonist who at first sees too little, then, as a growing consciousness of an expanding universe comes about by the very act of seeing, constituted as a form of voyeuristic *self*-consciousness, begins to see too much. The dilemma for James's protagonists in *What Maisie Knew* and *The Wings of the Dove* becomes one of fitting into the self-constituted picture, given that it is never complete or finished (consciousness, for James, stops only at death, and until then continuously reflects upon the limitations of its scope and the quantity of its blind spots). This redoubling or reflexive twist is equally present in those metacritical reflections of the prefaces where James positions himself both inside and outside the "picture" of a given novel, and worries about the extent of his survey both when he is within the picture, as author, and outside the picture, as critic.

For Haneke, the hyper-visuality of contemporaneity—cameras on every street corner—operates within the limits of a kind of presentism that depends upon a repression of the past. In relation to the novel in the hands of James, with its exposure of a voyeuristic consciousness increasingly aware of both what it can and can't see, the surveillance camera in the contemporary urban environment of Paris offers Haneke the perfect metaphor for an anxious society resting upon panoptic fantasies, obsessed with its own security, and indifferent to the safety and well-being of the "other"; indeed, in its anti-bourgeois, paranoid narrative, *Caché* makes it clear that the survival of the one depends upon the exclusion and extermination of the other. In the film, James's voyeuristic consciousness is translated into the optics of the camera which, however multiplied at every possible site in the pursuit of capturing everything (eyes at a countless number of windows) inevitably fail to "see" those blind spots—on the fringes of the social order, hidden in the past—upon which a panoptic construction of reality ironically depends. For both James and Haneke, as they etch the reflexive twist in their work, the limits of vision are engrained in the medium itself: the novel, as an inscription of consciousness observing itself seeing all that it can see and all that it cannot; film, the televisual, and the digital (all operating in *Caché* to produce visibility) as a registering of what the surveillance camera sees, all the time, proffering the panoptic fantasy of our capacity to see everything if the collectivity of cameras is sufficient (it is not) to the scale of the "all."

In chapter 4, James's "The Beast in the Jungle" and Christopher Nolan's *Memento* are brought together as bearing a Janus-like relation to the concerns in *What Maisie Knew* and *Kill Bill* with childhood, mortality, and passing time discussed in chapter 2. In James's story and Nolan's film, the reversible relation between memory and the future takes center stage. John Marcher, the protagonist of "The Beast in the Jungle," lives only in a future that awaits him as a memory of what will have inevitably occurred, the future perfect thus becoming a fated past.[32] But constantly living in the tense of the future perfect causes him to visualize a specific event that, in effect, will never happen; the event itself exists as a mere figure of speech, the envisioned "beast" that will pounce upon him unawares that will convert anticipation into fact. This story about visualizing the future itself then exists in the form of a memory of the future reverse engineered into a past that, for James, serves as a rubric for the authorial relation to story, or more specifically, the story to come in the future of his writing. The conceptualization of futurity to medium is also explored narratively and cinematically in *Memento*. The notorious exploration of short-term memory loss and the construction of a future "backwards" as the film intersperses sequences in reverse chronological order with memories that move forward in time underscores Nolan's reflection on film as a collation of cut and spliced time slices that enable a narrative relation to futurity. The future of the subject as well as the future of the medium (or more precisely, how the future can be represented narratively and cinematically) undergirds the "plots" of both the story and the film, to the degree that plot becomes a problem not to be solved by any narrational schemes. On the one hand, "The Beast in the Jungle" is a story about the man in time to whom nothing was ever to have happened; on the other, *Memento* is a film about a man who remembers nothing about what has happened to him in the recent past: both film and story plot this "nothing" as the content of their medium.

The nature of the reflexivity inherent in James's fiction and the films discussed up to this point, and its bearing upon questions of time, media, and authorial/directorial survey, lead to the central concerns of chapter 5: what is the nature of experience, and what is the comparable relation between experience and reality as mediated through the devices of a novel and the instruments of a film? A discussion of James's *The Ambassadors* and Hitchcock's *Rear Window* reveals that both author and director, engaged in narrativizing what a protagonist sees and understands when encountering an initially unfathomable event, provides complex reflections on the nature of event as such and the capacity of the medium of choice to render what happened in a time and space captured (or, more pointedly, trapped) within the confines of the mediation. Going back to claims made at the beginning of this introduction, this chapter offers a capstone assessment of how just "looking" in James and Hitchcock—an act enfolded in both the plots and materiality of their respective novels and films—signals modernity's investment in visuality as a primary form of knowledge, and knowledge as the scriptable and visual registering of consciousness in motion. We see, therefore we exist; we think, and what we think we see forms the content of what we experience. Clearly, this rubric has become intensified as we move into the digital age, but early on, Henry James had a sense of it, just as it would be adumbrated in the genre of film as it evolved. I thus conclude with a brief discussion of *Melancholia* and "The Beast in the Jungle" redivivus as imagining the limits and ends—the "felt ultimacies" as John Barth puts it in "The Literature of Exhaustion"—of the mediums they exemplify, predicated, from the beginning, on the limits of knowing, seeing, and experiencing.[33] My goal, throughout, is to assert the importance of close reading and close looking in assessing the encompassing issues of medium, genre, and thought upon which this book freely touches.

Chapter 1

Of Birds and Birdcages

"In the Cage" and *The Birds*

> Like a bird on the wire
> Like a drunk in a midnight choir
> I have tried, in my way, to be free.
>
> —Leonard Cohen, "Bird on the Wire"

Leonard Cohen's 1969 signature lyric posits a conundrum about freedom: I have tried to be free in my vocalizations, sings the Keatsian bird/drunk, but my freedom to sing has coincided with linearity, restriction, and conformity. In this chestnut of poetic complaint, form and the constrictions of the poetic instrument ("wire" referring to guitar strings) contend with spontaneity in the reproduction of the poet's song and soul, his "freedom." Notwithstanding Cohen's "I have tried" and "in my way" (those clichés of contemporary victimization), his image of a bird on a wire demonstrates what I want to define as a particular circumstance of modernity to be found in the first set of works I wish to discuss, "In the Cage," Henry James's deeply weird, voyeuristic novella of 1898 and *The Birds*, Hitchcock's 1963 epic of avian mayhem and the second of the trilogy of films—sandwiched between *Psycho* (1960) and *Marnie* (1963)—devoted to possessive mothers, bad daughters, and generally possessed adults. This circumstance can be characterized as the dually complicit and conflicted relation between the simulation and the putative freedom of the subject, which foments the illusion that the more the subject is redoubled, the more mobile it becomes. This relation rests upon an ambiguation of the ideology underlying what Herbert Schneidau has definitively explored in *Sacred Discontent* as the alienation of the modern Western subject—a double alienation in that it compounds the alienation of the subject in culture and inevitably represents it as the alienation of culture from nature, or the inviolate gap of the real existing between the social and the imaginary broached by modern self-consciousness.[1]

In drawing out this relation, the first question to be asked is why James and why Hitchcock on the specific question of the alienation of the subject? To begin, somewhat facetiously, as portrayed subjects, it is sometimes difficult to tell them apart, at least in profile. Both are portly modernists, bookends to an epoch, at least in the case of James on the front end if we follow Hugh Kenner's characterization of him in *The Pound Era* as the era's absent father, encountering the young Ezra and Dorothy in London while on a walk with his niece "toward the evening of a gone world," a meeting that Kenner characterizes as follows:

> "Mr. Pound! . . ." in the searching voice, torch for unimagined labyrinths; and on, to the effect of presenting his niece Margaret; whereafter Mr. Pound presented Mr. James to his wife Dorothy; and the painter's eye of Dorothy Pound, née Shakespear, "took in," as James would have phrased it, Henry James. "A fairly portly figure."
>
> Fifty years later, under an Italian sky, the red waistcoat seemed half chimerical—"that may be imagination!"—but let us posit it; Gautier wore such a garment to the *Hernani* première, that formal declaration (1830) of art's antipathy to the impercipient, and James would have buttoned it for this outing with didactic deliberation.[2]

For Kenner, whose treatise on modernism as a novel is modeled on *Ulysses*—thus the implicit comparison between the didactic, "stately, plump Buck Mulligan" of the novel's introit and the didactic, portentous Henry James shepherding in modernism by seeing out the short nineteenth century—James's "unimagined labyrinths" conspire with "art's antipathy to the impercipient" to produce a body of work that combines obsessive reflexivity and compulsive attention to detail.

We might also say the same of Hitchcock's films from, roughly, *The Man Who Knew Too Much* (1934 version) on, in that Hitchcock stands in proximate relation to the latter epoch of cinematic modernism as James stands in relation to the earlier epoch of literary modernism.[3] More pointedly, James and Hitchcock reflect in unprecedented ways on this relation. In both, detail and labyrinth—signature elements of their collective opus—entail a specificity that intensifies relative to the degree of reflexivity, thus signifying consignment of the real to the realm of the utterly indeterminate, marked above all by endless simulations of the factual, the reduplicative. Meanwhile, the work of the text, literary or cinematic, is rendered—in the auteur mode of "I have tried in my way"—as a mapping of social labyrinths through the accumulation and gathering of myriad details. For James, this dissemination and gathering occurs in the representation of intersubjective consciousnesses, the precision and particularity of "thinking" forging myriad mnemonic connections across time and space. For Hitchcock, they are conveyed through visual iconographies produced by framing and the intercutting of close-ups and wide shots, a vast field of birds of every species, birds on every wire, the eye and beak of a single bird as it attacks a terrified child, intimating the apocalyptic failure of culture's plot to rule nature. In both instances, I will suggest, the hidden agenda is to bolster a notion of human subjectivity impossibly escaping, via a sleight of hand, the net of reality by becoming paradoxically trapped in what James figures in the preface to *Roderick Hudson* as the skein of social "relations" that "stop nowhere," the "exquisite problem of the artist" being "eternally . . . to draw, by a geometry of his own, the circle within which they shall happily *appear* to do so."[4]

So much depends in James and Hitchcock on the perception of detail, on the ability to sort out between two or several equally valid logics which one is most consonant with "reality," or to exist, impossibly from the perspective of ideological critique, in both or all at once, though it is certainly pretty to think so. "Everything counts," writes James in the preface to his first novel, "nothing is superfluous . . . the explorer's notebook . . . [is] . . . endlessly receptive"; thus, an obsessive attention to every detail—what he describes as "the beguiling charm of the *accessory* facts in a given . . . case"—marks the high moment of revelation for many a James protagonist.[5] Similarly, for Hitchcock, as Tom Cohen remarks, we can observe the manner in which Hitchcock "turns film into a surface amalgamating a multitude of material and technological markers beyond the mimetic images," thus generating a cinematic text that operates via a host of myriad details to deflect our attention from the narrative, while signifying the same narrative's overdetermination.[6] As I noted in the introduction, in the odd figure he develops for his early work as an author for whom everything comes to count, James writes that as a "young embroiderer of the canvas of life" he

> began to work in terror . . . of the vast expanse of that surface, of the boundless number of its distinct perforations for the needle, and of the tendency inherent in his many-colored flowers and figures to cover and consume as many as possible of the little holes. The development of the flower, of the figure, involved thus an immense counting of holes and a careful selection among them. That would have been . . . a brave enough process, were it not the nature of the holes to so to invite, to solicit, to persuade, to practice positively a thousand lures and deceits.[7]

This lure of detail which, extending James's figure, is a fetishistic excrescence upon the grid of reality.[8] For James, what makes reality mesh, the net of its network, the parceling out of the big hole of the real into the "little holes" that constitute both its narratability and its being-narrated—this seduction by the nitpicky—intimates the larger investments of modernity in what Žižek in *The Ticklish Subject* terms the splitting of "the subject of desire" from "the subject of drive." The former, Žižek writes, is "grounded in . . . constitutive lack," whereas the latter—the subject of drive—"is grounded in a constitutive *surplus*, that is to say, in the excessive presence of some Thing that is inherently 'impossible' and should not be here, in our present reality—the Thing which, of course, is ultimately *the subject itself*."[9] In a preliminary sense, what is happening with detail in James and Hitchcock, what has transpired under modernity according to Žižek, who traces the split of the subject of desire and the subject of drive from Hegel to Badiou, is the evolution of identity as fundamentally voyeuristic, a way of seeing that we will witness repeatedly in the comparisons in this book between James and modern cinema. Voyeuristic identity in this formulation is a matter of filling in the blanks of an inconceivable totality by perversely observing the always suspicious acts of others and by assuming that the real action is always elsewhere, but only real if observed unobserved, or observing and observed with both parties feigning ignorance of observability.

This condition of the "impossible" modern subject has nothing to do with desire as such, but everything to do with the splitting of desire from drive and, analogously, within the more confined realm of modernist aesthetics, the splitting of the capacity for reflexivity from the capacity for representation. James worries about it in his preface to *Roderick Hudson*: you can never fill in all of those tiny holes, you can never see or know enough. In order to make "it" narratable, the author is driven, reflexively, to leave myriad gaps, and to exert a principle of selectivity that reveals as its significant aesthetic limitations as much as it enables one to write in the first place. Hitchcock has similar concerns: despite all of the clues, repetitions, doublings, details, symbolic and logical chains, and technological gimmickry of his films, the narratives themselves never add up, save as visual puzzles and iconographic fields. D. A. Miller puts it this way in discussing the continuity errors and red herring/McGuffin plots foisted upon a public looking for solutions to mysteries and film scholars looking for clues to hidden meanings in the offerings of the master of suspense:

> En bloc, the errors uncannily combine with the whole ethos of mistake, confusion, and nonsense that permeates Hitchcockian cinema, from its elaborate intrigues that never make sense on close inspection, to its perfectionistic protagonists foiled by slipups as little as a latchkey, to its general theology of original sin that puts everyone, and even everything, in the wrong. Hitchcock may not set out to commit a particular continuity error, but in his accident-driven Weltanschauung, any such error must be considered as waiting to happen, and when it does, feel not just stupidly out of place, but also eerily at home. These motley accidents, though narratively dysfunctional, have the odd capacity to bond, like open valences in chemistry, with stylistic motifs that lend them some of their own artistic necessity. Yet these bonds are wild, unstable; they neither facilitate stylistic homogeneity nor bring hermeneutic repose to the Too-Close Viewer who attempts to read them.[10]

Thus, *Vertigo* (1958), in which a man falls in love with and witnesses the death of the same woman twice, once for practice, once for real; *The Birds*, an essay on the apocalyptic incidental and accidental; *Psycho*, which argues that not only *can* you go home again, you can't go, nor have you ever been, anywhere else; *Rear Window* (1954), in which a man sees exactly what he sees, the point of the film being that he must convince others that he sees exactly what he sees. What you see in Hitchcock is what you get—a succession of loosely associated images reflecting his sense that life is an entirely metonymical affair, an endless procession of contingencies, images, objects, events, and persons. Both Hitchcock and James compensate for this narrative concern that drives their art: this sense that the more you immerse yourself in the texture and weave of detail, which is the only thing of interest to do in any case, the less sense it will all make, or in Žižekian terms, the closer you come to the Thing of subject, the more it vanishes before your eyes. Narrative itself, of course, conceived as drive pure and simple—its ends irrelevant and inaccessible in any case, is the solution to its own inadequacy. James writes, Hitchcock films; they construct hyper-reflexive stories and subjects in those stories who look everywhere for some Thing until they find or lose it. This compensatory strategy results in textual and cinematic narratives instantiating subjects whose desire is entirely constrained, in an oddly formal sense, by the very drive that is supposed to get us where we want to go, but only and always takes us where we've already been.

In typically Jamesian fashion, the story behind "In the Cage" is so insubstantial as to cause the reader to reflect ironically on its "aboutness," or the essential hole at the center of events fetishized with detail so that it has all of the appearance of being a great deal about something rather than nothing. The protagonist is an insignificant post office clerk whose dull life and prospects of a dull marriage to her fellow clerk and future grocer, the dully named Mr. Mudge, are elevated only at work, behind the cage of the telegraph counter, her position that "of a young person spending, in framed and wired confinement, the life of a guinea-pig or a magpie."[11] In her cage, she has the opportunity to observe how the other half lives as she checks the steady flow of telegrams being paid for by her rich customers before they are handed over to the telegraph operator. Privy to a network of communications between multiple parties entangled in the vast, but seemingly singular, web of circumstances that constitute the social order of late Victorian London aristocracy, "our young lady," as James refers to her throughout, stumbles upon a conspiratorial affair between one Captain Everard and a married woman, Lady Bradeen.[12] Because both are clients, James's protagonist is able to track the affair with its attendant covert meetings and coded messages that allow it to progress in a mode of "secrecy" that is obvious to everyone. Of course, behind the cage, taking his messages and returning his change, she falls in love with the aptly named Everard herself, but must live out her passion vicariously as the "friend" who facilitates matters in speeding the messages on their way and being a repository or registrar for all of the communications that have passed through her hands.

Our young lady is, thus, a hermetic figure, a voyeuristic message-sorter at the center of a narrative about sorting messages; as the telegraph clerk, she both purveys and purloins information—coding and decoding it—such that in her labor the relation between subjects and objects of knowledge is collapsed. Mark Goble has written of James's interest in an "aesthetics of communication" in his late novels that "explore the possibility of instantaneous communication over a distance" in various ways. Goble cites the proliferation of popular stories and novels such as Ella Cheever Thayer's *Wired Love: A Romance of Dots and Dashes* (1880) as evidence of an emerging minor genre—the techno-romance—which James "exploits with sometimes excruciating convolution."[13] Thayer's novel of a relationship between two telegraph operators conducted by code is quite different from James's story of a clerk in a telegraph office and her relationship with an upper-class customer who occasionally comes into to send messages, but both feature coding and telegraphic communication as important plot devices in narrating those relationships.

In her role as clerk, James's protagonist, who "had seen all sorts of things and pieced together all sorts of mysteries . . . had an extraordinary way of keeping clues."[14] The word "clue" is, itself, something of a red flag in James's fiction, suggesting, as here, that there is an indecipherable mystery for the reader/detective to attempt to unravel alongside James's (often clueless) protagonists, and we will see that flag being raised more than once in this study. With a scandalous affair at its center, "In the Cage" is replete with secrets and clues: our young lady is characterized has having a "hazard of personal sympathy" that enables her "to see more of" (the dangling preposition making "more of" what not quite clear) with a "vision for silver threads and moonbeams and her gift for keeping the clues and finding her way in the tangle."[15] More judgmentally, she is described as having "a sense of carrying . . . in her pocket" the "silly, guilty secrets of brazen women . . . whose squanderings and graspings, whose struggles and . . . love-affairs and lies she tracked."[16] Captain Everhard refers to the date of a fateful telegram he asks her to retrieve as a "clue";[17] to her friend, Mrs. Jordan, our young lady describes her rich clientele with *National Enquirer*–like zest: "Their affairs, their appointments and arrangements, their little games and secret vices—those things all pass before me."[18] Confined in her clerk's cage, she gains a kind of limited omniscience, a freedom to see and know everything that "passes" before her. In a story published just two years before "In the Cage," "The Figure in the Carpet," James had spun out a similar figuration between clues and cages when an aging writer lures a young critic into an obsessional fantasy about the buried "golden treasure" of a secret in his writing to be found if only the undiscovered clues in the collected work could be unearthed: " 'My whole lucid effort gives [you] the clue—every page and line and letter. The thing's as concrete there as a bird in a cage, a bait on a hook, a piece of cheese in a mouse-trap. It's stuck into every volume as your foot is stuck into your shoe. It governs every line, it chooses every word, it dots every i, it places every comma.' "[19] Here, and in "In the Cage," the paradox of confinement and free access to knowledge and information is formulated as the capacity to gather and decode clues visible only to those in the message-sorter's (critic's or telegraph clerk's) privileged position.

As she increasingly gathers "clues" about the Everard/Bradeen affair, she perceives herself leading a "double life . . . in the cage"[20]—that of the grocer's fiancée, the anonymous clerk, and that of one who is at the panoptic center of a global system of communication and exchange:

> As the weeks went on there she lived more and more into the world of whiffs and glimpses, she found her divinations worked faster and stretched further. It was a prodigious view as the pressure heightened, a panorama fed with facts and figures, flushed with a torrent of color and accompanied with wondrous world-music. . . . There were times when all the wires in the country seemed to start from the little hole-and-corner where she plied for a livelihood and where, in the shuffle of feet, the flutter of "forms," the straying of stamps and the ring of change over the counter, the people she had fallen into the habit of remembering and fitting together with others, and of having her theories and interpretations of, kept up before her their long procession and rotation.[21]

It is likely that only voyeuristically, in one who aspires to megalomania, could the bureaucracy of telegraphy be idealized in this fashion—that is, only if what is overseen, peeked at, or looked into can be woven into a systematic yet diffused narrative whose point is not the code but the coding, not the message but the glorification of the messenger. Like Mrs. Jordan, who has constructed for herself a boutique career as a floral arranger for the rich, James's protagonist "more than peeped in—she penetrated"; into the "immensity of th[e] intercourse" between her clients, she reads in "stories and meaning without end"; and, like a detective, she "tracks" "mainly in one relation, the relation as to which the cage convinced her, she believed, more than anything else could have done, that it was quite the most diffused."[22]

James thus confers upon his unnamed protagonist the power to assemble out of overwrought "clues," shreds of evidence, and sporadic messages (for her clients, including the beloved Captain Everard, frequently take their messages elsewhere) a "whole" narrative discourse that is both self-contained and scattered. It is both replete with "facts and figures" in a communication system where money and information are exchanged at an increasingly furious rate, yet so empty of content that the "real story" of "In the Cage" is not what the protagonist discovers—for she only finds out the whole story behind the affair second (voyeuristic) hand, from Mrs. Jordan, who "hears things" while arranging plants in mansions—but what she accomplishes as a kind of authorial stand-in who brings a putative totality to the semi-random, scattered, and partial fictions she "peeps into." Performance, not disclosure, is the sign of narrative "success" in James's tale.

The contradictions of our young lady's position are revealed in the novella's climax, when Captain Everard has reached a crisis point in his relationship with Lady Bradeen and visits the telegraph office to see if a copy has been kept of a telegram she has sent through a third party to him. Apparently, the original has fallen into the wrong hands, and though the pair have been careful to code their telegrams in such a way as to obscure references, Everard fears there is something in the message (or not in the message, it is not clear) that might give them away. Taken aback by Everard's imperialistic attitude in this tense episode, our young lady takes the opportunity to engage in some sadistic play with the captain, for though the copy of his telegram has been discarded long ago, she retains perfect memory of every message he has sent through her, but prolongs revealing her recollection to him while he squirms. She thus takes revenge upon him as part of her dawning recognition that:

a) after all, she is but a servant to him and the aristocratic world that he embodies, though her voyeurism has allowed her to imagine herself at its center, empowered as the gaze which sees it and controls the flow of its information from behind the cage;

b) she actually knows very little about Everard and his affairs;

c) the more she does know, or manufactures as known, the more she realizes the fragile, semi-accidental contingency of his story to hers. She is on the margins of his narrative, nearly invisible, which is why she must seize this fleeting instant when she becomes central to his destiny: "It came to her there, with her eyes on his face, that she held the whole thing in her hand, held it as she held her pencil, which might have broken at that instant in her tightened grip. This made her feel like the very fountain of fate, but the emotion was such a flood that she had to press it back with all her force."[23]

Only on rare occasions is James quite so frank about who holds or has the capacity to squeeze, manipulate, and even break the Thing, though it is obvious that for James the Thing is nothing, a constitutive surplus, as Eric Savoy argues in his reading of James's objects, in the register of synecdoche as fetishes that "gesture to an elusive, entirely imaginary, and unspecifiable wholeness."[24] Captain Everard explains that the telegram " 'fell into the wrong hands, but there's something in it . . . that *may* be all right. That is, if it's wrong, don't you know? It's all right if it's wrong.' "[25] His dilemma is that Lady Bradeen can't remember what she put in the message, so that it is not known if she put the wrong thing (an unintentional bit of disinformation) or the right thing (coded correct information). The latter, he fears, will provide a telling clue to whomever has intercepted the message about the nature of their relationship. What is actually contained in this purloined letter—what assignation it refers to, how the information it contains can be mapped or located within the array of circumstances to which the clerk believes she has full access—remains obscured. Finally letting him off the hook, after tortuous minutes in which she plays the role of "some strange woman at Knightsbridge or Paddington," she provides to Captain Everard confirmation that the original telegram contained a mistake in the form of a code written on the back of his card:

> He fairly glared at it. "Seven, nine, four—"
>
> "Nine, six, one"—she obligingly completed the number. "Is it right?" she smiled.

> He took the whole thing in with a flushed intensity . . . "By all the powers—it's wrong!" And without another look, without a word of thanks . . . straightened his triumphant shoulders and strode out of the place.
>
> She was left confronted with her habitual critics. "If it's wrong it's all right!" she extravagantly quoted to them.[26]

794961: what could it be? A date? It does not parse. A telephone number? Possibly, but it is a stretch given that in 1900, two years after the publication of "In the Cage," the London telephone system was still using simple four-digit numbers and did not have the need to move to a larger three-letter prefix and four-digit number system until the 1920s.[27] An address? A mathematical subroutine? A "cipher code," as John Carlos Rowe queries, potentially "as legible as the code cracked (complete with instructions) in Poe's 'The Gold Bug'?"[28] In terms of the narrative, it makes little difference what this vital piece of information actually refers to: it is pure code, pure "constitutive surplus," and the clerk's power lies in her ability to reveal or conceal it. Her mistake, however, is to think that she acquires some form of agency in the larger world outside the cage of class and reduced expectations because she controls the dissemination of partial or coded information.

Here, it is worthwhile to distinguish between power and agency, just as we must distinguish between drive and desire, for the postal clerk's function in both possessing and yielding up the code is remarkable for its disabled effects. Her position as telegrapher doesn't provide her with a larger view into the affair to which she has only a kind of hieroglyphic access (for narrative access—the only kind a true voyeur is interested in—she must rely on Mrs. Jordan). It has no effect on the outcome, for what would have happened or not happened as the result of the interception of the message has already happened or not happened, depending upon whether the message is right or wrong, in which case it's all right, and Captain Everard simply wants to find out how much trouble he is going to be or not going to be in as a result. Ultimately, her role as postal clerk completely and finally removes her from the realm of contingency to the social order that Captain Everard inhabits, for in the process of giving him the Thing, the code, she is reduced to the role of alien menial to the upper classes (the "strange woman at Knightsbridge or Paddington") rather than being confidante to the demi-gods of the London aristocracy. The delivery of the code reveals the extent to which her power as informant is reliant upon her position as a kind of switching mechanism in a digital system of communication and exchange, an operant whose province is limited to the bytes of information flowing through her, and only one of many such mechanisms which might be used, randomly or not, under given circumstances (as the narrative makes clear, Captain Everard and his ilk tend to deliver their messages at whatever local telegraph office suits their convenience). Our young woman's access to information—the quanta of her mobility as subject—is thus inextricably linked to her placement or entrapment in the cage/matrix of the social order. There is no agency here, but only a drive-function, a routing mechanism for desire in a situation where drive is, as it were, everywhere (there are untold thousands of messages screened by hundreds of such postal clerks in late nineteenth-century London every day), and desire—or what I will term *the narratability of drive*—is nowhere, nothing, the *aftermath* of drive.

The anonymous postal clerk's plight is that of the modern, post-Hegelian subject, or as Žižek states it, "the subject [that] is the very gap filled in by the gesture of subjectivization."[29] Enter stately, plump Alfred Hitchcock. *The Birds*, Hitchcock's forty-seventh feature film and arguably the one that, technically, posed the most difficulty for him, could be seen as an "In the Cage" expanded to global proportions.[30] The postal clerk's delusional centrism regarding her "little hole-and-corner" is blown up to gargantuan dimensions in *The Birds* as the cage of Bodega Bay comes under attack from fowls of all species whose presence is attributed to the arrival of Melanie Daniels (played by Tippi Hedren), a San Francisco socialite more of the order of Lady Bradeen than our young woman. Melanie comes to the fishing village in order to play a practical joke on a man she has just met in the city, Mitch Brennan (played by Rod Taylor), and ends up staying for dinner and much more. As is the case with James's novella, one wishes to ask what this film is about, beyond surplus of detail: so many birds, so many Things flocking together, that even in their specificity (one or two crows per child in a scene where children are attacked in a schoolyard) they become indistinguishable, a single big Thing, a parliament of fowls acting in concert, orchestrated by forces unknown as it comes out of the sky at random moments portending the end of the human world. *The Birds* was released only months after the Cuban Missile Crisis at the height of the Cold War, but whether the narrative of the film can be read allegorically as the self-destructiveness of technology with its bird-missiles raining down without warning out of the sky, or as the revenge of nature on culture, closer to the script's origins in the Daphne du Maurier's story, is somewhat moot.[31] For *The Birds*, I contend, is not primarily about Cold War paranoia, scapegoated women, nature's revenge, the racializing of evil, or animal superiority, though all of these themes are registered as such in the film's tangle of contending and partial narratives.

To be sure, there are scenes, in which we witness two stunningly beautiful actors (Hedren and her co-star, Suzanne Pleshette) playing characters who are castigated by the local community for their "difference" and who are physically violated by birds/rapists, conceivably as an element of the all-too-familiar cinematic trope that figures outspoken and sexually aggressive women (both are both) as scapegoats and victims.[32] The "end of the world" aura of the film, its setting in a remote coastal location that has *On the Beach* (novel, 1957; film, 1959) written all over it, and its ending as its survivors wander, zombie-like, through a landscape covered with birds of assorted species, clearly suggest that the film is "about" a localized form of nuclear holocaust. Invading clouds of black birds descending on the white community of Bodega Bay and, in particular, violating the body of the rich Melanie Daniels suggest that racial paranoia is at least partially behind what is going on in the film. Perhaps more directly, multiple scenes in which a non-threatening, seemingly pastoral bird or two becomes a mob of vengeful animals descending on humans seem to echo all of those ecological disaster flicks that have been with us and have proliferated with abandon since *Godzilla* (1954). Many of these, like *The Birds,* depict nature, animals, or machines trumping the human, such that one way of viewing the film is as an embodiment of a prescient posthumanism. These thematic strands, and many others, are woven into a film that seems to be both about everything and, allegorically, about nothing in particular—that is, it is an allegory of particularity, or symptomaticity per se. To employ James's metaphor of the embroidered "canvas of life," reality in *The Birds* is only comprehensible as a series of holes or gaps to be filled in; a thousand gulls and black birds coming suddenly out of the sky as a manifestation of that sheer contingency writ large that we struggle to organize into a narrative of something, anything.

In effect a pastiche, *The Birds* is encyclopedic in its fetishistic detail and its provision of partial, compensatory narratives that attempt to explain what is happening in a film where nothing is happening except sheer event, the Big Other's surprise attacks on the humble citizenry

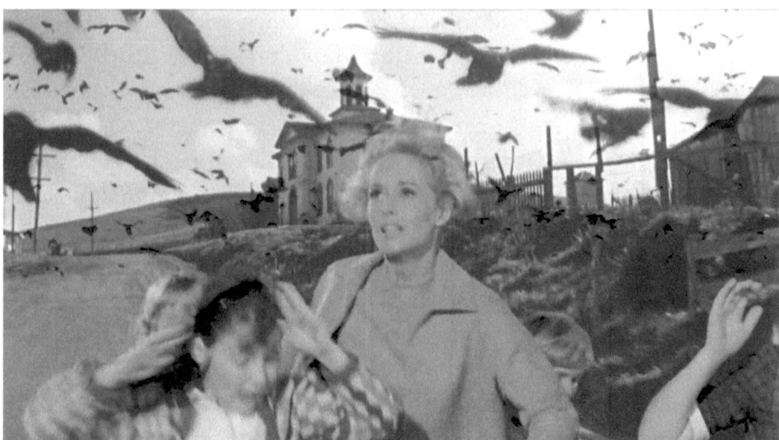

Figure 1.1. Fleeing the plague of fowls in *The Birds*. *The Birds*, Universal Pictures, 1963. Frame capture courtesy of Joshua Yumibe.

of the planet.[33] In one of the film's key scenes, taking place at The Tides restaurant where Melanie has sought refuge after the most recent bird attack on the town's schoolchildren, opinion and information are exchanged offering leads to an explanation for events, but they—and all the other leads the film offers—are red herrings, dozens of inoperative codes changing hands, as if Hitchcock had decided to enact a reprise of all of his McGuffins in one film. What is, in effect, a town meeting in the local hangout (and a message-sorting scene writ large, the solitary perspective of the telegraph clerk in her cage made communitarian), turns into a parodic theatricalization of the social order attempting to cope with that which lies completely outside the range of its narrative methods and compensations. An elderly citizen attempts to explain how it is impossible for birds of a different feather to flock together; a fishing boat captain angrily denounces an unprovoked assault upon his vessel by epic gulls/albatrosses; a drunken bar patron, announcing the apocalypse, quotes scripture; but none of these logics—scientific, mythological, theological—offer any real purchase upon the question of what has gone wrong in Bodega Bay, and why. In a flurry of reference, visual puns, and general hermeneutic excess, we see children, fearful that the birds are going to eat them, eating fried chicken; we hear two citations from the Old Testament and one from the New; we witness expert testimony on the difference between blackbirds and crows, the size of bird brains, the flocking habits of fowls, and the numbers of birds and species in North

America and the world; we see a bevy of signs and details—multiplied liquor bottles on the wall, two matches lighted to ignite one cigarette (a foreshadowing of the bird attack in the next scene, where the man having the scotch at the bar drops a lighted match while getting into his car that ignites a trail of spilled gasoline causing a spectacular explosion of cars and gasoline pumps), the "no credit" and "no checks accepted" signs, the Gallo wine sign, the reversed neon sign in the bar window, the Bodega Bay welding sign across the street, photos of Bodega Bay and impressionistic paintings of rural scenes, the cigarette machine with its mirror that reflects the waitress's movements, and the symmetrically arranged ashtrays lined up at the bar. Hitchcock's set decoration in this scene is thus an elaborate assemblage of seemingly random but, actually, carefully curated elements that gesture in multiple directions toward the destructiveness of modern "life" in its habits and technologies. And then there are the stereotyped roles and guises of the bit actors in this scene: the drunken prophet; the neurotic mother; the salty captain telling tales of monsters at sea; the amateur ornithologist/detective Miss Bundy, sticking to the facts and looking for all the world like Miss Marple; the cynical outsider. One can attribute all of this excessive, hyperbolic detail and referentiality to "realism" or the weaving of plot, but it is all provided, here and everywhere in *The Birds*, to activate an intention behind the eruption of the real in the film instantiated by the bird attacks—an intention that never arrives or hits its mark.

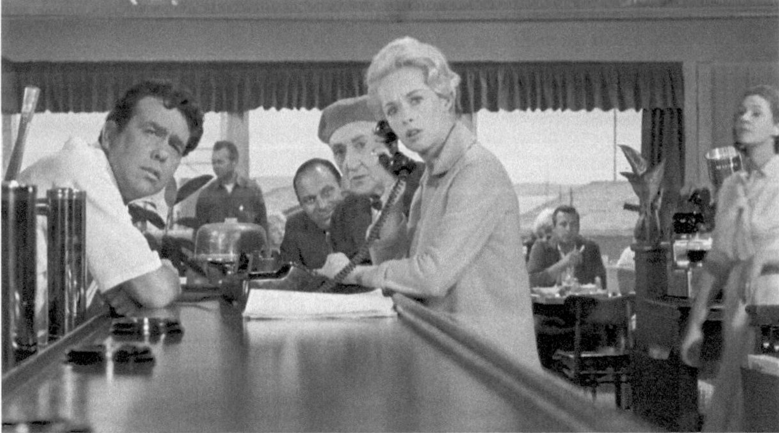

Figure 1.2. Listening to the prophet at The Tides restaurant. *The Birds*, Universal Pictures, 1963. Frame capture courtesy of Joshua Yumibe.

The film does invite explanation, as if it needed to elicit from the viewer the ontological foundation for its own making, but the list of possibilities, from which I select a few highlights, is self-contradictory and fragmentary. *The Birds* offers no motive or reason for itself, no explanation, whole and intact, for the events—planned or random, orchestrated or merely "documented"—screened therein:

1. Melanie Daniels is an evil, alien presence who consciously or unconsciously brings destruction to the rural landscape with her from the big city (San Francisco), representing the corruption of nature by culture in modernity. Humankind has angered an anthropomorphic nature by ignoring, exploiting, or caging it (the film begins in a San Francisco pet shop; Melanie comes to town bearing caged love birds; Bodega Bay is a fishing village, etc.), and the film portrays nature's just anthropomorphic revenge.

2. A paranoiac subset of one: Melanie Daniels is a reformed embodiment of *la dolce vita*—a rich girl, having once been falsely accused of running through fountains in Rome in the nude, she now does volunteer work for children (figuratively, the same ones attacked by the birds) and takes a course on general semantics at Berkeley (yet she's the worst reader in the movie: the student of the human science that studies the formation of meaning is, at every turn, speechless or tautological when confronted with the question of what it all means). Though she's changed her life (here, Hitchcock's Catholicism comes into play), she's guilty forever, and the film is "about" the eternal exacting of retribution and scapegoating for one's past sins.

3. It's an anti-smoking movie! (Drinking is bad, too.) Melanie Daniels smokes incessantly during the film, lighting up twice with Mitch's old girlfriend, Annie Hayworth, the local schoolteacher. Melanie is smoking outside the schoolyard as birds assemble to attack the children, and drinking martinis with Mitch just before they attack children at a birthday party. And then there is the punishment exacted upon the man at the bar for lighting up a cigar—he gets

blown up and burned to death. In fact, eating, smoking, drinking, sex, and talking in general are regarded in this film as punishable behaviors. All, of course, can be read as assaults upon nature, illustrative of the nature-versus-culture thematic of the film—but nature conceived as what? If everything other than any form of human social interaction is nature, then nature is a kind of zero, since the film makes it clear that "nature" is a series of representations emerging from the social imaginary. The birds, on the other hand, are aberrations of the natural order; or rather, in this narrative where the flocking and squawking of birds serve as parodic embodiments of the human, and where the violence and appetites of humans, always on display, serve to demonstrate our base, birdy nature, the birds represent the self-cancellation of the social order, human desire hoisted by its own petard.

4. It's all about the (postmodern) Oedipus complex where everybody must get castrated. Mitch Brennan can't be released from Mom's (Jessica Tandy's) clutches (what might be called in other terms her Oedipal attention span) until he undergoes the trials of manhood that includes bringing Melanie home to roost and protecting the family keep. We see his victory when Lydia, returning in horror from a neighbor's farm where she has seen a corpse with its eyes pecked out, drives up to the house to see Melanie and Mitch in what is clearly a post-coital embrace, she dressed in flannel nightgown (bought from the local general store) and fur coat (a remnant of her days of Roman decadence). As Mitch and company drive out of paradise in a final, apocalyptic scene where the sun sets over birds covering the landscape as far as the eye can see, a shocked, wounded Melanie, visually raped by a flock of birds, lies in the sympathetic arms of that tough old survivor bird, Lydia Brenner, her gaze now directed at her new (re-castrated) daughter and away from her (post-castrated) son, her Oedipal attention now "properly" redirected. The nuclear family is redeemed, re-nucleated, though in an asymmetrical way: son becomes dad (who died years ago,

> and whose picture is shredded by the birds when they attack the family homestead); the bad mother becomes the good mother; the bad, rebellious daughter becomes the good, supplicant (raped) daughter, though there is the curious twist in that Lydia now has two daughters, e.g., a surplus of daughters and no sons, unless one counts Mitch reconstituted as both castrated son and father now that the threat of the castrating daughter is out of the way.

The laundry list explanations, intentions, interpretations, and motives could go on, but none of these result in a total logic or economy that can be said to undergird the film. The birds in *The Birds* are for nothing and no one, or for everything and everyone; they are both just birds and avatars of everything from the coming apocalypse and Russian missile strength to nature, guilt, the sublime, the other to technology's other, the exteriorization of the Oedipal, and the reinternalization of the exteriorization of the drive per se. This movie is what happens, to invoke Žižek again, when the subject of drive is split from the subject of desire, or when constitutive surplus is delinked from constitutive lack; that is, it portrays the formation of modern subjectivity as an attack on subjectivity, or more precisely, subjectivity under attack from itself. This is not the "divided self" of existentialism nor the split subject of classic Lacanian analysis; it is not the celebrated mobile subject of happy postmodernism nor the paranoid subject of sad postmodernism; it is neither the ethnic subject nor the white subject; it is neither regional nor global; it is neither imperialized nor imperialistic. Or, rather, it is not only one of these, and more than all of them at once. Much as we might wish to ordain alterities to this subject, it is the sign of its limits that a "correct other" is all too easily reincorporated into the voracious reflexivity of the subject in which desire is riven from drive. All of these are symptomatic features of modern subjectivity per se, which among other things is to be recognized as a series of semblances in which the ratio between constitutive surplus and constitutive lack is negotiated symptomatically.

As I intimated at the beginning, viewing "In the Cage" and *The Birds* as symptomatic "bookends" to modernity reveals the trajectory of the modern subject as fundamentally voyeuristic, though different voyeuristic logics exist between the author and the filmmaker. Certainly, some of these arise out of intermedial differences, especially if one accepts the standard tenets of post-1960s film theory regarding film viewing and filmmaking as implicitly voyeuristic; but I am concerned here with a conception of subjectivity that has found its medium in film, but that is by no means coterminous with that medium. As we have seen, the protagonist of "In the Cage" is literally voyeuristic: she lives her life—her only life, for it is clear that marriage to Mr. Mudd and removal to the London suburbs is, for her, a form of death—through the messages exchanged between amorous parties; she studies the semiotic codes of the aristocracy in order to spy out and play a role in their affairs in the only way she can, as a switch point in a system of communication and exchange. The postal clerk's voyeurism involves peering through the screen of code to the events beyond she perceives as being experienced by others, but of course this activity is an integral part of a larger system of proliferating urban semiosis and commodification (a telegraph station in every neighborhood; a computer in every home) that can only operate by means of subjects occupying the position of voyeur. Spying on the rich in "In the Cage," an occupation engaged more forthrightly by Mrs. Jordan, who overhears much as she places flowers on the dining tables and sideboards of the wealthy, is integral to the ongoing work of the social order of pre-Fordist capitalism represented in the novella, for such voyeurism symptomatically recirculates the desire for status, wealth, sex, and beauty that structures that order. But equally important, James makes clear, is the absolute separation of this system's "drive"—the flow of information and gossip, the libidinality of class envy that motivates our young lady's momentary sadism in withholding information from Captain Everard—from the desiring subjects existing within it. Our young lady's subjectivity, reduced to the consciousness of a desire that can only locate its objects "secondhand," accidentally or contingently, becomes a function that exists entirely within the cage of the workplace, and only by virtue of the information she spies passing through her hands.

In *The Birds*, the world of "In the Cage" is turned inside out, for the voyeurism of Hitchcock's film resides entirely in the eyes of the birds and the bird's-eye of the camera, as if the semiotic surplus of the drive was looking to the specific and localized play of desire for its energy, its constitution. One spectacular sequence in the film can serve as a reflexive example of how the entire film sees itself. As the birds attack the townspeople of Bodega Bay with ensuing explosions, wrecked cars, broken windows, and general mayhem, the camera suddenly telescopes out and we see the town from far above, over the shoulder, as it were, of the hovering birds, viewing the drive to meaningless violence and global destruction at its source. It is as if, gazing on the social order through the lens of the vertical cinematic mobility Hitchcock deploys for this bird's-eye (or god's-eye) shot, everything will become clear, narratively and visually. But this inverted voyeurism merely serves to confirm, spatially, the gap between the birds as embodiments of "sense-less" drive and the surplus of intentionality it magnetizes as the humans, below, enact their mythemes, practice their hermeneutics, and perform amazing escapes from and reattachments to the embodiments of Oedipal desire. Subjectivity, in this scenario, is the attempt to elide the violence of the separation between the constitutive surplus of the drive and the constitute lack of desire by discerning its logic which, if nothing else, offers the illusory predictability of the return of that violence upon itself, in the subject. *The Birds*'s excess and fetishizing of detail and action represent the degree to which drive has separated from desire in this realm where information has replaced knowledge in a narrative that commences with a scene of commerce (the purchase of lovebirds in a gilded cage) that leads, both inevitably and by hook or crook, to a scene of apocalypse now.

In his "First Prelude" in the *Introduction to Modernity*, Henri Lefebvre considers the mode of modern historical being as that of "maieutic irony." Reading Marx's famous passage from "The Eighteenth Brumaire" on repetition and revolution in history, Lefebvre writes that

> from the basis of what is determined, history creates the unforeseen; it never repeats itself; and nothing demonstrates this better than its pseudo-repetitions. For Marxists, the Hegelian cunning of the idea in history becomes the objective irony of history acting within subjectivities. This irony comes from the fact that "men," social forces and ideas, masses and individuals, act in ways contrary to their intentions; and moreover, they express their actions by ideologies, signs and symbols which are frequently misleading. Sooner or later even the best-laid plans will come to grief; such is the law. There is always an element of the unforeseen in history, even though history is not absurd, devoid of meaning, undetermined. The foreseen and the unforeseen, chance and necessity—these are the constituents of dialectical movement in history, and doubtless in nature too; the determination of becoming.[34]

Regarding this dense formulation as symptomatic rather than constative, we might ask how it is that a revealing conception of modernist subjectivity in history could arrive at the notion that "social forces and ideas, masses and individuals" have achieved an ironic status in which they can "act in ways contrary to their intention." Where does this counter-intention come from? How do we, in mass or individually, register this contrariety? How do we know we are acting contrary to intention, and not just intentionally acting contrarily? Such questions could only be posed toward a definition of semi-free historical subjectivity (contrary to Lefebvre's intentions, I am sure!) in which the split within the subject between drive as constitutive surplus and desire as constitutive lack has already occurred *in* history. Certainly, in these narratives by James and Hitchcock, we encounter the question of how it is possible for acts and events to occur contrary to intention, at the crossroads of contending intentions, and at the extremes, without intention or without occasion altogether. The putatively free modern subject, existing as the gap that exists between desire and drive, constitutes itself, like capital, as a singular embodiment of lack and surplus. This subject has too much freedom, and too little agency; it is replete with intention confronting a totality, a "real" that offers only contingency—even "terror," to use James's word—as the reward for confronting its monolithic presence. This is the return of the subject as a form of illusory singularity—"a bird on a wire"—to its true home in modernity, infinitely multiplied, and always the voyeuristic observer of its own nefarious agency.

Chapter 2

Childhood Living

What Maisie Knew and *Kill Bill*

The previous chapter explored object relations, voyeurism, and the totality of representation in James's "In the Cage" and Hitchcock's *The Birds*. In this chapter, I will focus on issues of temporality, childhood, and the structuring and destruction of experience in James's sexual free-for-all for Victorian adults, *What Maisie Knew*, and Quentin Tarantino's postmodern chronicle of corporeal mayhem and a free-for-all of another kind in *Kill Bill: Vol. 1* and *Vol. 2*. In the unlikely comparison of James to Tarantino, it is instructive to observe how the experience of time and the relation of that experience to mortality is present in the work of a modernist writer whose exploration of perspective and the partiality of individual vision is still being worked out on film. What is being worked out between *What Maisie Knew* and *Kill Bill* is a specific relation between time and experience, and the primary purpose of this chapter is to investigate how this relation is registered narratively and cinematically. Both James and Tarantino ask: What happens when the ratio between experience and temporality is skewed, when there is an overexposure to the end of experience in mortality? And both locate this conundrum in the figure of the child, whose ephemeral existence is only and always conceived as a passing away before time.

Kill Bill is a film about wasting time, the wasting away of temporality, the time of wasting bodies, landscapes, and cinematic repertoires. It is a film that envisages the serialization of the historical, as if history was simply a pure succession of events marked by the afterglow of their consummation. Pertinent here is Harry D. Harootunian's observation that, for Walter Benjamin, the construction of history is essentially performative, seeking to "produce a certain concrete effect, the coming together of the Then . . . and the Now . . . into a constellation like a flash of lightning."[1] The notion of history as composed of constellations that link the past and present in a series of simultaneities or instantaneous conflations of past and present is clearly in opposition to all historicisms that posit eternal successions or reich-like continuums extending into the far reaches of time. This is a notion to be differentiated as well from what Giorgio Agamben refers to as the "dead time" of modernity; that is,

> the representation of time as homogenous, rectilinear and empty [that] derives from the experience of manufacturing work and is sanctioned by modern mechanics, which establishes the primacy of uniform rectilinear motion over circular motion. The experience of dead time abstracted from experience, which characterizes life in modern cities and factories, seems to give credence to the idea that the precise fleeting instant is the only human time. Before and after, notions which were vague for Antiquity—and which, for Christianity, had meaning only in terms of the end of time—now become meaning in themselves and for themselves, and this meaning is presented as truly historical.[2]

Even though the formation of historical constellations may be instantaneous, Benjaminian temporality relies, precisely, on the *linkage* of "then" and "now"—a linkage that is not preordained, nor eschatologically integrated into some grand narrative of progress. As Agamben suggests, it is the forging of the relation between "then" and "now," or "before" and "after," that is critical to the construction and representation of an authentic historicity. Here, Agamben is not referring to a simple notion of causality, but to a complex relation in which the multiple paths between past and present are continuously traversed—the traversals, themselves, integral to the notion of experience. For Agamben, an authentic relationality between past and present offers a resistance and alternative to the forms of experience legislated by modernist temporalities of the instance, given over to "the imposition of a form of experience as controlled and manipulated as a laboratory maze for rats."[3] "When the only possible experience is horror or lies," he states, "then the rejection of experience can provisionally embody a legitimate defense."[4] What Agamben refers to as "the destruction of experience," in other terms, has the potential to open a rupture in the narratives of fatal progress or fascistic instantaneousness that may allow us to re-experience the full temporality of history in the present.

The *Kill Bill* films envision the destruction of experience under the paternal regime of destinal time disguised as, simply, a matter of the moment. They do so by substituting for this regime one given over neither to the law of the father (Bill's law) nor to symmetrical logics of reproduction that would reinstate the nuclear family romance that Bill has both destroyed, through a sheer display of sadistic willpower, and seeks to restore, through a sheer display of sadistic willpower. As I shall show in a reading of *Kill Bill: Vol. 2*'s penultimate scene and, then, in the key scene of *What Maisie Knew* where Maisie is stirred into a murderous passion by the indomitable Mrs. Wix, this substitution comes in the form of the irresolvable contradiction of the child who appears to be radically innocent, a "little unspotted soul,"[5] as Maisie is described, yet who is at the same time a homunculus whose knowledge of corruption and mortality, *in potentia*, is complete. For Maisie, the experience of being a child takes place in the temporal void of time occurring before its time as she is interred in the "tomb . . . of childhood," [6] according to James's catachrestic figure.[7] Symptomatically, in the *Kill Bill* films and *What Maisie Knew*, a certain conception of temporality—the time between infancy and adulthood—is without content, merely a vacuum or switch point: the girl-child, Maisie, is frequently referred to as "old man" by her debonair stepfather, Sir Claude, implicitly collapsing the time of the child into that of the adult, as well as swapping out her gender. In *Kill Bill*, childhood is usually portrayed not as a state of being but as the instant when the child crosses over into adult knowledge—an instant brought on by the witnessing or infliction of violence and the voiding of life. Both James and Tarantino portray childhood as a kind of temporal black hole or non sequitur that occurs as an afterthought to the apprehension of mortality most visibly located in the transience of the parent.[8]

❧

In the *Kill Bill* films, multiple temporalities are brought into conjunction with each other as the narrative unfolds in the films' frequent backtracking and hyper-citational excess: the anachronism of the Old West in Tarantino's riff on the spaghetti westerns of Sergio Leone and Sergio Corbucci; the hyperkinetic, metonymical redundancies of an actional present in Tarantino's take on the Hong Kong action films of Chung Sun and John Woo, and as prettified by Ang Lee; the samurai films of Kurosawa, Inagaki, and Fujita drenched in a weird temporal mix of the medieval and the futuristic; the psychosexual melodramas of Roman Polanski and Kim Ki-young, the latter the cinematic mentor of Park Chan-wook whose "vengeance" trilogy is roughly contemporaneous with *Kill Bill*; and briefer asides to the 1950s retro postmodern domesticity of David Lynch, the Hitchcockian variations of DePalma, the frenetic and blood-drenched *noir giallos* of Bava and Argento, and motorcycle movies from *The Wild One* to *Easy Rider*.

Beyond providing a four-hour quiz for genre buffs, the encyclopedic assemblage of the *Kill Bill* films subverts the notion of a dominant temporality because, in a sense, no time, no diegetic extrapolation lasts long enough to establish itself as having a past to its present, a future to its past. In effect, the *Kill Bill* films are a cinematic pastiche, an effect achieved through Tarantino's seemingly random assemblage of takes from different shot angles and the centrifugal energies generated by a constant flow of citations of other films and genres. The films thus enact, in Mary Anne Doane's phrase, an "epistemology of contingency" spun out of control; that is, one in which the presence of the spectator can no longer provide the assurance of a unified event, the "structuring of contingency" given over to the profusions of spectacle which, according to Doane, paraphrasing Laura Mulvey, is "fundamentally atemporal, associated with stasis and the antilinear."[9] What is particularly relevant in this formulation to the phantasmagoria of the *Kill Bill* films is Doane's insistence that the cinematic structuring of contingency into event—something that occurs between image and spectator—takes place as a relation to mortality: experience, in this view, comes about within a temporal continuum with an eye, as it were, toward death. Yet, primarily in *Kill Bill: Vol. 1*, which might be viewed as the spectacle ancillary to *Kill Bill: Vol. 2*'s event, death is so ubiquitous that it ceases to be the end point of events—the effect related to cause—rendered through the structuring of contingency that constitutes conventional notions of plot and chronology. *Kill Bill: Vol. 1* can be viewed as merely composed of spectacles of death—individualized, as when the heroine, The Bride, aka Beatrix Kiddo, scalps and slays O-Ren Ishii in a Hiroshige-like winter garden; or on a massive scale, when she kills or maims all of the members of Ishii's entourage and every single one of the Crazy 88s at the House of Blue Leaves nightclub.

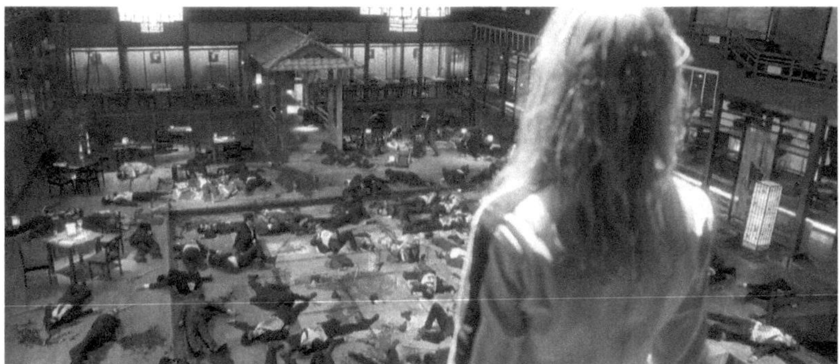

Figure 2.1. Beatrix observing the massacre of the Crazy 88 at the House of Blue Leaves. *Kill Bill,* Vol. 1, Miramax, 2003. Frame capture courtesy of Joshua Yumibe.

Interspersed amongst the killing scenes are the fragmentary minor narratives that serve as the symptomatic routings that get us from one spectacle of blood sprays and body parts to another. The relation between the two films (which were once meant to be one) is that of X-ray to diagnosis: the symptomology of *Vol. 1* is transformed into the explanatory narrative of *Vol. 2*. Observing more carefully the relation between spectacle and *récit* will allow us to come to terms with the *Kill Bill* films' incorporation of a temporality whose fallout offers revisionary, if parodic, versions of experience and event.

The elaborate explanatory arc that one can trace across the two films tells us that because she has, supposedly, broken the heart of Bill, a "murdering bastard" (as he calls himself) and Manson-like leader of the Deadly Viper Assassination Squad, Beatrix, along with the entire wedding party and church staff, has been left for dead by the DiVAS at her own wedding rehearsal taking place in a desert chapel somewhere near El Paso. In the several expositions occurring primarily in *Vol. 2* via flashbacks and the long conversation between Bill and Beatrix in the finale, we learn that Beatrix has left because she is pregnant with her guru/father/lover's baby and, understandably, feels that rearing a child while working for a group of assassins might be problematic. Beatrix's disappearance is enabled when she informs a female contract killer about to blow her apart with what looks like a portable cannon that she is with child. The killer (a mother herself?) agrees to let bygones be bygones, thus reversing the scenes in which Beatrix is forced to kill Vernita Green seconds before her child enters the room to see her corpse, or the anime representation of O-Ren Ishii's parents being executed, samurai-style, before her eyes while she hides under a bed. When Beatrix drops out of sight, knowing that Bill would never simply give her permission to leave, Bill assumes that she has been killed. On the track of her assumed killers, he discovers that she is, indeed, alive, working in a record store in El Paso, and about to be married. Enraged at what he perceives as her betrayal, he orchestrates her death at the wedding chapel, and personally shoots the bullet that he thinks will kill her into her head. A millisecond before dying, in the instant between that when Bill pulls the trigger and when the bullet enters her skull, she whispers that the child is Bill's. This scene is repeated as the establishing sequence for both volumes of the film.

The attack places Beatrix in a coma for four-and-a-half years, from which she is awakened by a mosquito bite; somehow, while comatose, she has managed to give birth to her daughter, and Bill has managed to kidnap the child and raise her on his own. The rest of the film's narrative is given over to the succession of vengeful attacks Beatrix attempts to carry out on the four members of the DiVAS, and, finally, on Bill himself. There are several noteworthy aspects of the films' narrative successions. First, the assassination attempts are not presented in the order they occurred in time—we see the killing of Vernita Green before the slaying of O-Ren Ishii, though the latter occurred first; in *Vol. 2*, we see the killings of Budd (Bill's brother), Elle Driver, and Bill in chronological order, but as in *Vol. 1*, the killings are disrupted by flashback sequences that offer, once more, fragmentary explanations for how "then" became "now." Secondly, the extended flashbacks of both volumes are, in effect, stories of origin and ontology: how O-Ren Ishii came to be an assassin after witnessing her parents' execution by mobsters; how Elle Driver became a one-eyed assassin; how Beatrix was trained by super-guru Pai Mei and thus learned the exotic karate move that allows her to kill Bill; how Beatrix escaped an assassin and left Bill in an attempt to become a bourgeois subject. These origin stories of mentoring and childhood experience always occur as brushes with death: the memory of childhood and pedagogy are thus conflated with the scene of mortality, lending weight to the idea that childhood itself in *Kill Bill* is but a de-temporalized point of transition from an amorphous "before time" to a "now" where all learning is equated with the either/or of mastery or victimization. As I've previously suggested, the narrative de-temporalization of the *Kill Bill* films is bolstered visually by the films' fragmenting of the relation between time and space via its citations: now, a citational reference suggests, we are in the Old West, and in the next instant, in a postmodern technocracy, or the Japan of the Edo period. Interestingly, no scenes from Beatrix's childhood are portrayed in the film. She appears to be just, as Bill terms her, "a natural born killer" who has been mentored by Bill as a twenty-something assassin, a master of death, and who, perhaps, seeks to recuperate a vestigial childhood by repossessing her daughter, thus saving her from her own fate. But as we shall see, the pathos of Beatrix's reunion with her daughter is complicated by the fact that, symbolically, the child has already crossed over into territory of mortal knowledge that marks, for both James and Tarantino, the representational limits and "contents" of childhood per se.

Along with the profusion of temporalities and temporal shifts to be observed in the *Kill Bill* films, these explanatory mini-narratives, set alongside the extended scenes of bloody battles, spectacular assassinations, and martial arts exhibitions, underscore the severe mismatch in the films between event and spectacle, or "history" and experience, if we consider the former as the narratable content yielded by the latter. For none of these narratives provide any basis for the hyperbolic effects they produce. Thus, it seems relatively reasonable for Bill, in David Carradine's master-to-grasshopper voice learned while serving time as a warrior-pupil in the *Kung Fu* TV series, to suggest in the closing scenes of the film that he was merely overreacting to the runaway bride's perfidy in murdering an entire roomful of people and shooting the woman pregnant with his child in the face. Overreacting, yes, but just a little, given that he is ontologically a "murdering bastard." The effect of these disconnects, overdeterminations, and affective imbalances is to produce a severe rupture in the "before" and "after" of the films diegesis, and thus, as Agamben suggests, to posit a destruction or deconstruction of experience as something that exists in a temporal continuum in relation to death. There is, as it were, an overabundance mortal experience in these films related in accounts that are not even close to being settled by narrative content; there is, on the other hand, a profusion of temporalities that cannot add up to an historical continuum or set of contingencies that could allow experience to be meaningfully framed.

One sequence, in particular, illustrates the contradictions that I have just described, especially as they come rest in the condition of the child. Near the end of *Vol. 2*, Beatrix, planning to surprise and take her revenge on him, walks in on Bill in his condo in Mexico playing with their daughter. In a series of sequences that veer wildly between domestic sentimentality á la *Father Knows Best* and domestic violence involving pointed guns, swords, and a truth-serum dart, several mock and real death scenarios are discussed and played out. Excerpts from the train of conversations between Beatrix, Bill, and B.B. (the child) that take place during this fatal family reunion reveal to what extent death is on everyone's mind:

> (Bill and B.B., playing cowboys as Beatrix enters)
>
> B.B. (toy gun in hand): Freeze, Mommy.
>
> Bill: Bang, bang! Oh! Oh! She got us, B.B. Mommy got us. Oh, I'm dying! (groaning) I'm dying. Fall down, sweetheart. Mommy shot us.
>
> Bill (sotto voice): But little did Quickdraw Kiddo know that little B.B. was only playing possum, due to the fact that she was impervious to bullets.
>
> B.B. I am 'pervious to bullets, Mommy.
>
> Bill: Hey, get back down there. You're playing possum.
>
> Bill (sotto voice): So, as the smirking killer advanced on what she thought was a bullet-ridden corpse, that's when little B.B. fired.
>
> B.B.: Bang, bang! You're dead, Mommy. So die.
>
> Beatrix: Oh! B.B. Oh! B. B . . . (grunts). I should've known. You are . . . the best.
>
> B.B.: Oh, Mommy. Don't die. I was just playing.
>
> Beatrix: I know.
>
> Bill: I told her that you were asleep, but that one day you'd wake up and come back to her.

☙

(Later, as Bill makes sandwiches)

BILL: You know, sweetie, Mommy's kinda mad at Daddy.

B.B.: Why, Daddy? Were you being a bad daddy?

BILL: I'm afraid I was. I was a real bad daddy. Our little girl learned about life and death the other day. Wanna tell Mommy about what happened to Emilio?

B.B.: I killed him.

BILL: Emilio was her goldfish.

B.B.: Emilio was my goldfish.

BILL: She came running into my room, holding the fish in her hand and crying, "Daddy. Daddy. Emilio's dead." And I said, "Really? That's so sad. How did he die?" And what did you say?

B.B.: I stepped on him.

BILL: Actually, young lady, the words you so strategically used were, "I accidentally stepped on him." To which I queried, "And just how did your foot accidentally find its way into Emilio's fishbowl?" And she said, "No, no, no. Emilio was on the carpet when I stepped on him." Mmm. The plot thickens. "And just how did Emilio get on the carpet?" And Mommy, you would've been so proud of her. She didn't lie. She said she took Emilio out of his bowl and put him on the carpet. And what was Emilio doing on the carpet?

B.B.: Flapping.

BILL: And then you stomped on him.

B.B.: Uh-huh.

> BILL: And when you lifted up your foot . . . what was Emilio doing then?
>
> B.B.: Nothing.
>
> BILL: He stopped flapping, didn't he? She told me later that the second she lifted up her foot and saw Emilio not flapping, she knew what she had done. Is that not the perfect visual image of life and death?[10]

There is much of interest in the reunion sequences portraying deaths and mock deaths imagined, remembered, confessed, and prophesized. Daddy and daughter pretend to be shot by Mommy, and daughter (who is impervious to bullets, like Daddy's favorite superhero, Superman) plays possum; daughter pretends to kill Mommy, who pretends to die; daughter prevaricates about accidentally killing her goldfish, Emilio, and then confesses she intended to do so; Daddy (who is the real father of one daughter in the room and the symbolic father of the other) tells daughter about how he tried to kill Mommy/daughter, with the explanation that he was a "bad Daddy" then, but has changed because the event made him sad and brought him to understand the irreversibility of time. After this discussion, Mommy and daughter watch a samurai film, *Shogun Assassin* (1980), a postmortem pastiche of Kenji Misumi's Lone Wolf series, in which a samurai warrior's wife is killed by his paranoid shogun master; seeking out the master, the betrayed pupil goes on the road with his toddler son, engaging in mercenary work along the way so that he can support his two-unit family until he finds and kills the shogun and his three Masters of Death. Minutes after the video is over and daughter is asleep, Mommy will go into the living room to be "shot" by Daddy with a truth serum dart that initiates a flashback to how Mommy escaped Daddy's clutches in the first place by playing possum. Finally, Mommy and Daddy have the ultimate showdown in which Daddy really is killed by Mommy, but the death is portrayed in such a way that it is almost as if he is just sleeping, just lapsing into unconsciousness, which is what Daddy told his daughter Mommy was doing when she was in the coma induced by Daddy's failed attempt to really kill Mommy as the result of Mommy's pretending to be dead.

In these scenes, what has up to this point been a matter of spectacle is now converted into conversation, indicating that the film is attempting a performative feint to match experience with event, but the "match" is merely a bevy of repetitions, fake gestures, temporal disconnects, tautological statements, and Dr. Seuss revelations: trying to kill Mommy made the bad dad sad. What is the result of this attempt to diegetically represent the destruction of experience that the film has heretofore portrayed through its slapstick proliferation of visual acrobatics, jump cuts, shufflings of genre, and temporal disruptions? One answer is that, in this narrative array, the paternal war machine has been utterly sundered, the master replaced by the pupil, Daddy replaced by Mommy, and the paranoid symbolic order (one that instantiates the void of childhood, just as Bill attempts at the earliest age possible needed to sustain the illusion of naturalness to induce in his child a catechism of mortality) replaced by a semiotic order of reproduction, protection, and the timely acknowledgement of beauty-in-life that exists solely between mother and daughter.

Countering this reading, there is the fact that Mommy and daughter are watching a particularly violent cartoon at the film's end (one in which magpies are being hunted by an insane Elmer Fudd–type), they have fallen asleep in each other's arms while viewing *Shogun Assassin*, and there is the hint that the daughter has inherited the mother's "natural born killer" gene with the stomping of her goldfish. Yet again, one might argue that all of these are displacements of the "real violence" that permeate the film signifying a directorial inquiry into the capacity of the cinematic image to convey "real" violence in the first place. Tarantino's completely over-the-top, metacinematic sequencing continuously quotes and parodies death and killing sequences from, seemingly, every available genre. No "realism" is possible in these films that are so thoroughly cartoonish, overdone, and hilariously exaggerated at every turn. Even the exception of the twinned establishment sequences that show The Bride's battered face in grainy black and white can be viewed as self-aware quotations of all of those movies that alternate fantasy sequences in color with "realistic" sequences in monochrome, as if the entire film were given over to "disproving" its own initiatory realism. Does the overkill of citation and affect suggest that the murderous "he" has simply become a kinder, gentler, but equally murderous "she" in *Kill Bill*? And has the acknowledgement of death-in-life, the marker of childhood's end, become a matter of sheer repetition, the film itself merely a masturbatory, pornographic assemblage composed of dozens of reenactments of the repetition compulsion? Or perhaps there is transformation here: the transformation of spectacle into discourse; the movement from some form of paternal to some form of maternal order that is analogous yet different, signifying a displacement of the law of violence and a different relationality that could reinstitute the temporality of childhood as content and continuity between "then" and "now." The film's indeterminacy in this regard—it's straining against its own logic in attempting to introduce discursive difference, paradoxically, via the mode of repetition—reveals the degree of its ironic discomfort with both its content and methodology (simulation), including those simulations of childhood innocence predicated upon a prior state of existence in which the subject is fully present to itself. One might call this contemporary knowledge, deadly serious in its smartass acting out.

❧

The disturbing, over-the-top visual violence of *Kill Bill* offers startling similarities to the equally disturbing rhetorical violence of *What Maisie Knew*. As J. Hillis Miller has suggested in his reading of the novel's figurations of voice, *What Maisie Knew* is, in part, about the acquisition of knowledge and how such acquisition takes place in the intersubjectivities of reader, narrator, and protagonist. For Miller, the very partiality of knowledge induces an interpretive crisis leading to action; thus, Maisie, who "sometimes . . . knows without knowing she knows; sometimes . . . knows and knows she knows; sometimes . . . thinks she knows but does not know; sometimes . . . knows she does not know," is driven by the slowly clarifying opacity of her knowledge to decide not to live with her beloved stepfather if he will not end his relation with her stepmother.[11] As John Carlos Rowe has shown in detail, what Miller views as an education in subjectivity resulting in an ethical vision takes place within rapidly shifting cultural and political circumstances: "What does emerge as a crucial part of Maisie's education in the novel . . . is her encounter with a whole set of social ambiguities surrounding the classification of human beings according to artificial categories such as race, class, gender, sexuality, nationality, and age."[12] Arguably, Maisie's education, which proceeds with the first words of the novel and even before, in the preface, where James speaks of Maisie's "small expanding consciousness," spells the death of childhood, or more precisely, the end of the temporality that the child would otherwise have occupied.[13] One could conclude from *What Maisie Knew* that such is the case, for the "tomb of Maisie's childhood" figured in the novel's opening scenes suggests that from the beginning she is "abandoned to her fate" as a child who has irretrievably lost a childhood that she has never possessed.[14] Yet, with this grave beginning, the question arises: what temporal space (if not that of childhood) does Maisie occupy in a novel where she is also not yet an adult? Where is "she" in a world in which her only access to knowledge is via adults who are unfailingly duplicitous, and whose sense-making capacities pursue the logic of "any combo will do," thus serving as an ongoing enactment of the negative capability of the ethical decision?

Or perhaps a more relevant question: what does Maisie think of the mess of adult experience and behavior she witnesses stroboscopically throughout her young life? The plot of this novel of adultery is relatively straightforward, as it traces the peregrinations of a child turning toward adolescence while she observes the manners and misdeeds of the upper-class British social order, localized in the parental neglect and, ultimately, abandonment she suffers as they pursue "business" and amorous adventures. What *could* Maisie be thinking about the funny games taking place before her eyes as she is used as a negotiating chip between her parents, Beale and Ida Farange? How does she view the tug of war between the governess hired by her mother, Miss Overmore (later known as Mrs. Beale), who will become her stepmother in time, and Mrs. Wix, hired by her father, and the only real mother she has? How is she to regard her stepfather, Sir Claude, who marries her mother and then falls in love with her stepmother? The substitutive assemblage of parental figures to whom Maisie is exposed is observed in alternating episodes of confusion and enlightenment by the growing child, witnessed with increasing consternation by that embodiment of the parental fort-da, Mrs. Wix, impossibly in love herself with Sir Claude. Here, the substitutional logic of repetition evident in the killing scenes of the *Kill Bill* films becomes the substitutional logic that informs Maisie's relationship with every adult she come across as possible parent or parent replacement. Maisie is the coin of the realm in these scenarios, passed from one hand to another as the currency of false legitimacy; or, as James characterizes her in the preface to the New York Edition of the novel, the victim of parental "malpractice," a "wretched infant" who is "practically disowned, rebounding from racquet to racquet like a tennis-ball or a shuttlecock."[15] The whole fragile, incestuous arrangement comes crashing down in Boulogne-Sur-Mer, where Sir Claude has fled with Maisie and Mrs. Wix in the vain hope that everything will sort itself out, and where Maisie determines that she will live with none of her parents, real or surrogate, in whatever combination and under whatever conditions—legal or adulterous—they might contrive; she returns to England under the protection of Mrs. Wix. Maisie thus opts out of serial parenthood and the substitutive logic of adult, heterosexual relationships she has observed with the increasing sense that everyone will eventually couple with everyone else, ad infinitum, thus making them, positionally, all them same.

One of the differential comparisons that can be made between *Kill Bill* and *What Maisie Knew* is that while the former is all action and performance, the latter is all thought and theory. Experience exists in *Kill Bill* as self-consuming spectacle, whittled down to the quiddity of the immediate gesture in the fabled temporal collapse of postmodernity (instant adult! just add death!), while in James's novel the issue is not the destruction of experience, but the capacity to apprehend and structure experience perceived through a succession of immediacies in the time and mind of the child who has always already ceased being so. As Sharon Cameron has written in her superb study of thought in James, *What Maisie Knew* is most pointedly about "the limitations of consciousness," which are "intrinsic, with tension arising from the shifting barrier between consciousness and repression."[16] For Cameron, the novel is about thinking—consciousness—in general, Maisie's child-mind offering a specific and symptomatic occasion to observe the aforementioned barriers and tensions. Reading the novel in light of James's preface to the New York Edition, Cameron argues that both the novel and the preface demonstrate "the *deficiency* of consciousness, its inadequacy to apprehend the reality it needs to," though they "also predicate different causes to account for that insufficiency.[17] That is, while James, in the preface, asserts "that Maisie's consciousness has limits in terms of the child's sentimentalized innocence" and that blindness and insight for her are "externally generated by what others conspire to keep from her or by what she us unable to understand," the novel itself is invested in seeing the limits of Maisie's understanding "in terms of the dynamic relation between consciousness and unconsciousness," "contingent on what she *will* know, in the sense of having volition to."[18]

If we direct Cameron's insights toward the question of experience in time—to refer to Agamben once more, the experience legislated by modern temporalities of the instance—the question of how and what Maisie knows in the way that she knows things, as a series of scattered illuminations separated by days here, six months there, or merely seconds in the rapid-fire exchanges that characterize the novel's climatic scenes, becomes one of structure and position. To some degree, Maisie is engaged in an elaborate game of connect the dots, and in this regard, whether things are connected, or disconnected, or both at once, is queried repeatedly in the novel:

> Miss Overmore, then also in the vestibule, but of course in the other one, had been thoroughly audible and voluble; her protest had rung out bravely and she had declared that something—her pupil didn't know exactly what—was a regular wicked shame. That had at the time dimly recalled to Maisie the far-away moment of Moddle's great outbreak: there seemed always to be "shames" connected in one way or another with her migrations.[19]

> Another day, in another place—a place in Baker Street where at a hungry hour she had sat down with him to tea and buns—he brought out a question disconnected from previous talk. "I say, you know, what do you suppose your father *would* do?"[20]

> "Oh yes—there are plenty of trains." Again Sir Claude hesitated; it would have been hard to say if the child, between them, more connected or divided them. Then he brought out quietly: "It will be late for you to knock about. I'll see you over."[21]

> In the evening upstairs they had another strange sensation, as to which Maisie couldn't afterwards have told you whether it was bang in the middle or quite at the beginning that her companion sounded with fresh emphasis the note of the moral sense. What mattered was merely that she did exclaim, and again, as at first appeared, most disconnectedly: "God help me, it does seem to peep out!"[22]

> Mrs. Beale, at table between the pair, plainly attracted the attention Mrs. Wix had foretold. No other lady present was nearly so handsome, nor did the beauty of any other accommodate itself with such art to the homage it produced. She talked mainly to her other neighbor, and that left Maisie

> leisure both to note the manner in which eyes were riveted and nudges interchanged, and to lose herself in the meanings that, dimly as yet and disconnectedly, but with a vividness that fed apprehension, she could begin to read into her stepmother's independent move.[23]
>
> Sir Claude looked at his watch. "I had no idea it was so late, nor that we had been out so long. We weren't hungry. It passed like a flash. What *has* come up?"
>
> "Oh that she's disgusted," said Mrs. Beale.
>
> "With whom then?"
>
> "With Maisie." Even now she never looked at the child, who stood there equally associated and disconnected. "For having no moral sense."
>
> "How *should* she have?" Sir Claude tried again to shine a little at the companion of his walk. "How at any rate is it proved by her going out with me?"
>
> "Don't ask *me*; ask that woman. She drivels when she doesn't rage," Mrs. Beale declared.
>
> "And she leaves the child?"
>
> "She leaves the child," said Mrs. Beale with great emphasis and looking more than ever over Maisie's head.[24]

The rhetoric of connection and disconnection is fully located in Maisie as a maze of ignorance and/or knowledge in the last passage. She "stood there equally associated and disconnected," as if her identity and consciousness is equivalent to the degree to which, over time, she has been able to compute ratios of similarity and difference in her observations of her various parents' speech and acts. In this regard, as a fictional consciousness, Maisie is engaged all along in something like profiling, save that, in James's description in the novels closing scenes, she is, herself, the embodiment of the relationalities she perceives, seeing and seen become one, self-knowledge merged with the apprehension of the associations and disconnects between words and events to which she is constantly exposed.

In short, as Miller perceives, Masie's is the moral education of a reader. But beyond this, Maisie's experience of reading the reality around her, her coming to consciousness—a process that involves, as Cameron tells us, her repression of what she must repress, and her avowal of what she must avow—occurs within the temporal framework of a childhood that has, once again, ceased to exist with the novel's opening scene. There, an anonymous "good lady," discussing with Ida Farange the fact that Maisie will be exposed to countervailing narratives of her parents during her annual six-month rotation with each, exclaims " 'Poor little monkey!' . . . and the words were an epitaph for the tomb of Maisie's childhood."[25] The scene can be bookended with one at the opposite end of the novel, when several years have passed and Maisie is now, on a literal level, nearing the end of her phantom childhood. Touring Boulogne with Mrs. Wix, the pair engage in one of a series of elaborate conversations in which the governess is attempting to find out how much Maisie knows in order to find out what Maisie might do as a consequence of her knowledge. At this point in the narrative, Sir Claude fully occupies the position of Maisie's father as both Beale and Ida Farange have completely abandoned the child. Mrs. Beale occupies a more ambiguous position: her vanity, selfishness, and superficiality well qualify her for the wicked stepmother role that has also been played out by Maisie's biological mother. But she is also the former governess and the would-be stepmother redoubled to Maisie that she could be if Maisie would only accept the arrangements of the ménage proposed to her, whereby she would live as a daughter with Sir Claude and Mrs. Beale, who would be unmarried and in continental exile until they are married, if ever.

Mrs. Wix asks Maisie if she is jealous of Mrs. Beale, and when Maisie confesses that she has been, "lots of times,"[26] Mrs. Wix opines that Sir Claude is afraid of his paramour. Upon this revelation, Maisie gloomily reflects on how little she appears to really know Sir Claude, the most important person in her life at the moment: "Was the sum of all knowledge only to know how little in his presence one would ever reach it?" she asks herself, thus reiterating the negative ratio of the diminishment of knowledge in relation to the passing of time.[27] But this momentary interrogative and its attendant recognitions pass away quickly with the following exchange:

> The answer to that question luckily lost itself in the brightness suffusing the scene as soon as Maisie had thrown out in regard to Mrs. Beale such a remark as she had never dreamed she should live to make. "If I thought she was unkind to him—I don't know *what* I should do!"
>
> Mrs. Wix dropped one of her squints; she even confirmed it by a wild grunt. "I know what *I* should!"
>
> Masie at this felt that she lagged. "Well, I can think of *one* thing."
>
> Mrs. Wix more directly challenged her. "What is it, then?"
>
> Maisie met her expression as if it were a game with forfeits for winking. "I'd *kill* her." That at least, she hoped as she looked away, would guarantee her moral sense.[28]

This is not the first time that Maisie has been involved in such games with Mrs. Wix. Earlier, as a silent party to a conversation between Mrs. Wix and Sir Claude in which her governess pleads with her stepfather to become Maisie's protector, Maisie is portrayed as having "a sharpened sense of spectatorship" born of "long habit, from the first, of seeing herself in discussion and finding in the fury of it—she had a glimpse of the game of football—a sort of compensation for the doom of a peculiar passivity. It gave her often an odd air of being present at her history in as separate a manner as if she could only get at experience by flattening her noise against a pane of glass."[29] Moving from voyeuristic witness to interlocutor in the conversation with Mrs. Wix in Boulogne, we can view the promise and threat to kill, characterized as Maisie's perverse access to "moral sense," the fulfillment of the epitaph written upon the tomb of her childhood. The "poor little monkey" has now become, at least in this rhetorical game of diminishing returns, the potential murderer, the high moment of her education—a series of disconnected recognitions about how little she really knows—resulting in a performative declaration of a will to kill. At the same time, of course, the drastic remark, which "she had never dreamed she should live to make" as the resultant of her living, is all part of a game, accompanied with winks and grunts and dares not to wink, and a final looking signifying her arrival at an ironic point beyond childhood, where kidding is no longer kid-ding.

There are some remarkable similarities between this scene and the goldfish confessions of *Kill Bill.* Both involve discussions of murder within the context of an elaborate series of feints and gestures: a rhetoric of play located in facial expressions and intonations, a game about killing that could or is about to become real. But equally notable are the visible differences between these mortal games. In James, the game produces a consciousness of death at the limits of childhood, a consciousness of limit per se, reflected in Maisie's turning away as an avowal that the game is no longer just a game. Indeed, her childhood has been nothing but limit, an ironic counter-version of *bildung* or staged progress to adulthood because Maisie has always experienced knowing as a lightning-like illumination of not-knowing (to extend Miller's formulation, what she does not know, what she should not know, what she cannot possibly know, and what she cannot possibly not know), always in the discontinuous present. In Tarantino, the game produces not consciousness but a prefatory performance of death, which suggests that futurity is also a revisualization of the present, and that mortality is both the content and end of narrative. In slightly different terms, what is an epistemological problem for James (what can one know if the experience of modern temporality is that of being constantly at the limit of the present?) is a diegetical problem for Tarantino (how can narrative end, how can it be killed off, in a time of pure seriality, where instances are indistinguishable from each other, and where the pastiche of visual citations could continue *ad infinitum*?).

Both James and Tarantino locate these matters of time and narrative in portrayals of children confronting the limits of life and knowledge as the content of childhood. For both, childhood is a marker of the ratio of time to knowledge, the nature of the temporality they explore inextricably tied to the genres in which they work: James, via reflexivity, which produces the contents of consciousness; Tarantino, via cinematic simulations, which serves as the backdrop for sheer performance. Both represent temporality as replete with the discontinuity of its own successions and ends, and experience in time registered only as aftereffect, at the limit of time passing. Under such conditions, as Maisie knows, one can only "learn and learn and learn" until, as she parses it to herself, one reaches the limit always present in the first instance of learning: "condemned to know more and more, how could she logically stop before she should know Most?"[30] In slightly different terms, to play upon Mrs. Beale's maiden name, as James clearly intended, what is the limit to knowing "over more"? But what could "Most" possibly be in the game of never-ending substitution that both the novel and the film engage, and which Maisie here conceives as pedagogy? How can these narratives possibly end? Maisie goes back to England with Mrs. Wix; born again twice and having perfected her craft, Beatrix the assassin retrieves her child from her murderous father. Both pairs navigate toward a time and a future not discerned by the narratives in which they operate, for there is no externality to the limits made most visible in the elaborate geometries of substitution and repetition that undergird both *Kill Bill* and *What Maisie Knew*. James's exploration of childhood living reveals the impossibility of full closure as a kind of narrative limit, registered cinematically in Tarantino's film as an endless proliferation of dead bodies and a child who is heir to that logic. Both push the envelope of their respective medium to suggest the irresolution of time and continuity. In what might be viewed as an example of seriality attempting to escape itself, we witness the metonym of denucleated, same-gendered couples traipsing off into territories these narratives will not take us, and thus the possibility of a rupture that offers the potential for a different relation to time that Agamben imagines as another history. Beyond or most, however, appear as thoroughly reflexive rhetorical gestures that convey continuance as equivalent to *caesura* in these mortal stories that James and Tarantino firmly locate within the realm of the living, thus acknowledging the experience of mortality as the main event in life as we know it.

Chapter 3

Frame-Up

James, *Caché*, and the Borders of the Visible

In both "In the Cage" and *What Maisie Knew*, observing protagonists observing is at the heart of the narrative, as it is in all of James's late fictions. Both "our young woman" and Maisie labor under the rubric of surveillance as a means of knowing along with the meager access to power that being in the know brings. Surveillance is both the obverse and the limit-case of voyeurism, the universal extension of its optic investments. Surveillance hollows out the eye's desire in voyeurism; the surveillance camera sees everything that it is programmed to see only instrumentally, its eye mechanically trained on its object with no awareness, consciousness or intention "behind" it. While voyeurism retracts back onto the viewer, its danger, surprise, and affect wrapped up in the anticipation of the seer being seen, surveillance is entirely centrifugal. The surveillance camera has no interest in being seen; its primary function to keep its seeing hidden, except in those cases where it is clearly out in the open as a preventative to crimes that might have happened had the camera not been there. For James, a novelist primarily interested in representing what might be seen through the eyes of delimited subjectivities, the kinds of surveillance I have just described might seem of little interest, yet as we have seen in the countercurrents of the "house of fiction" metaphor, he is concerned about the artist's inability, literally, to see everything. For James, who began his career as a realist and concluded it by writing narratives characteristically permeated with paranoia, deceit, illusion, and suspicion, questions pertaining to the powers and capacities of observation have always been interrelated with his precepts about the artist's capacities and limitations in seeing everything that should be seen. That "should" is the clue that reveals both James's aesthetics and his ethics as a writer.

The problem for James is always one of seeing too much or too little. Žižek gives us insight to this problem as one related to modernity's knowledge about how observation works, which inheres in the act of visualizing per se, whether doing so in terms of an unfolding field of optic possibilities as described in "the house of fiction," or doing so for the sake of establishing mise-en-scène. For Žižek, the reflexive glitch induced by embodiments of modern visuality that formally and materially worry about the provenance of envisioning can be conceived as a "parallax," or

> the apparent displacement of an object (the shift of its position against a background), caused by a change in observational position that provides a new line of sight. The philosophical twist to be added . . . is that the observed difference is not simply "subjective," due to the fact that the same object which exists "out there" is seen from two different stances, or points of view. It is rather that, as Hegel would have put it, subject and object are inherently "mediated," so that an "epistemological" shift in the subject's point of view always reflects an "ontological" shift in the object itself. Or—to put it in Lacanese—the subject's gaze is . . . inscribed into the perceived object itself, in the guise of its "blind spot" . . . the point from which the object returns the gaze. . . . Materialism is not the direct assertion of my inclusion in objective reality (such an assertion presupposes that my position of enunciation is that of an external observer who can grasp the whole of reality); rather, it resides in the reflexive twist by means of which I am myself included in the picture constituted by me—it is this reflexive short-circuit, this necessary redoubling of myself as standing both outside and inside [the] picture, that bears witness to my "material existence."[1]

Looking in the rear view mirror provided by Žižek's Heisenbergian perspective, the Jamesian metaphor of the "house of fiction" can be regarded as a prescient metafictional commentary on the artist as onlooker that renders untenable the notion of "an external observer who can grasp the whole of reality" in an edifice replete with an indeterminate "number of possible windows not to be reckoned" which, by virtue of their multitudinous existence, serve to frame "the individual vision and . . . the pressure of the individual will."[2] James, once more, envisions the windows as claustrophobically disconnected "mere holes in a dead wall," and behind each, "a figure with a pair of eyes, or at least with a field-glass," all "watching the same show, but one seeing more where the other sees less, one seeing black where the other sees white, one seeing big where the other sees small, one seeing coarse where the other sees fine."[3] While James appears to take some comfort in the fact that this radically relativistic and indeterminate view of perspective and witnessing takes place against the backdrop of a common, singular, homogeneous "show," Žižek emphasizes in his description of the parallax the short circuit, gap, or shift in perspective inherent in acts seeing and observing objects in motion that produces a visualizing agency—the subjectivity who witnesses, watches, records—in the first place.

In this chapter, I will explore more fully how the parallax view operates in James via an examination of *The Wings of the Dove*, *What Maisie Knew*, and his prefaces to *Roderick Hudson* and *The Golden Bowl* and, correspondingly, Michael Haneke's 2005 film about the cinematic medium and the enabling or disabling powers of observation, *Caché*.[4] For both, countervailing acts of surveillance and voyeurism serve to limn subjectivity as seeing and seen. But first, a brief reprise of the implicit contradictions of representation and visualization that were, for James, according to R. P. Blackmur, "a torture, a care, and a delight" as he wrote the prefaces to the 1909 New York Edition of his novels and the late fiction that precedes them.[5] For Haneke, we will see the extent to which these incongruities are indicative of the material boundary that I mentioned in the introduction from Tom Gunning's description of the film medium: "the transparent" yet phantasmatic "nature of film . . . its status as a filter of light, a caster of shadows, a weaver of phantoms. . . . [where] the act of seeing encounters a bizarre entity whose quasi-ethereal nature marks the limit (or contradiction) of visibility."[6]

The optic parallax that Žižek describes is present in several registers of James's writing that can be gathered under the rubric of antinomy, a rhetorical gesture often ascribed to the general work of irony in his fiction, which James deploys to express the utter contradictions of human consciousness he observed. Specifically, antinomy, which has its etymological origins in the Greek "*anti*" "*nomos*" or "against the law," refers to an ambiguity in the law, following Kant's invocation of the concept in *The Critique of Judgement.* Antinomy has been viewed as a form of paradox in which two equally valid statements contradict each other, and yet, because both are valid, each must be allowed to stand as authentic or truthful under the law. In *The Critique*, Kant asserted that antinomy ruled the capacity of "reflective judgment," that is, the need to classify and order objects in the world so that they could be known according to principles generated subjectively via the language of statement in a kind of circular logic, thus serving as the means to authenticate the "truth" of the known object: *a* is knowable as belonging to the category of *b*, and *b* is knowable as the category that contains all of the *a*'s. The tautological nature of the reflective judgment—which he absolutely needs in order to complete a philosophical system that comprehends the "all" of reality in both its relativity and transcendence—spells trouble for Kant:

> But the *reflective* Judgement must subsume under a law, which is not yet given, and is therefore in fact only a principle of reflection upon objects, for which we are objectively quite in want of a law or of a concept of an Object that would be adequate as a principle for the cases that occur. Since now no use of the cognitive faculties can be permitted without principles, the reflective Judgement must in such cases serve as a principle for itself. This, because it is not objective and can supply no ground of cognition of the Object adequate for design, must serve as a mere subjective principle, for the purposive employment of our cognitive faculties, *i.e.* for reflecting upon a class of objects. Therefore in reference to such cases the reflective Judgement has its maxims—necessary maxims—on behalf of the cognition of natural laws in experience, in order to attain by their means to concepts, even concepts of Reason; since it has absolute need of such in order to learn merely to cognize nature according to its empirical laws.—Between these necessary maxims of the reflective Judgement there may be a conflict and consequently an antinomy, upon which a Dialectic bases itself. If each of two conflicting maxims has its ground in the nature of the cognitive faculties, this may be called a natural Dialectic, and an unavoidable illusion which we must expose and resolve in our Critique, to the end that it may not deceive us.[7]

This might be viewed as Kant's parallax. The trouble here is that the snake of duplicity and illusion has been inevitably introduced into the garden of pure reason, and though Kant proposes a method for dealing with it, by exposing it through critique (as if mere exposure were sufficient to "resolve" the contradiction residing like a black hole at the very heart of reflective judgment), it is not at all clear how two utterly opposed, but equally valid, maxims produced by the self-identical capacity of reflective judgment could possibly be synthesized in Kant's system.

The antinomies evident in James's fiction and prefaces tend to be caught up in his anxieties about the epistemological limitations of what his brother, William, termed "personal consciousness" in his 1892 lecture, "The Stream of Consciousness," in which the description of subjectivity and intersubjectivity eerily prefigures what Henry would say about the matter in the "house of fiction" metaphor:

> In this room . . . there are a multitude of thoughts, yours and mine, some of which cohere mutually, and some not. They are as little each-for-itself and reciprocally independent as they are all-belonging-together. They are neither: no one of them is separate, but each belongs with certain others and with none beside. My thought belongs with my other thoughts, and your thought with your other thoughts. . . . The only states of consciousness that we naturally deal with are found in personal consciousness, minds, selves, concrete particular I's and you's. Each of these minds keeps its own thoughts to itself. There is no giving or bartering between them. . . . Absolute insulation, irreducible pluralism, is the law. . . . Neither contemporaneity, nor proximity in space, nor similarity of quality and content are able to fuse thoughts together which are sundered by this barrier of belonging to different personal minds. The breaches between such thoughts are the most absolute breaches in nature.[8]

Citing the antinomious law of "absolute insulation, irreducible pluralism," William James introduces a notion of subjectivity as knowable only as a pure difference, a breach in consciousness (each its own singular window in the house of fiction) that incorporates the contradiction of individual consciousness as both utterly separate and self-identical and yet in intersubjective bondage at the same time. For Henry James, the intersubjective dimension of this formula is present in the notion of the "the spreading field, the human scene," or in other terms the commonly shared and available "reality" that each voyeuristic watcher observes from his or her own "hole" in the blank wall framing the house's many windows. Yet the liberating conceptualization of consciousness that validates the perspective of each witness to the human scene makes it, in its totality, unknowable save as a set of partial, often contradictory and incommunicable views that reveal the irremediable breach constituting the knowledge of the whole of reality as such.

This concept of consciousness increasingly informs the complexities and anxieties of knowing and envisioning in James's fiction as it evolves, and as he reflects on his authorial career in the prefaces. In the previous chapter, I discussed *What Maisie Knew* as a tale of dangerous childhood knowledge. For the purposes of the present discussion, it is worth considering how the act of knowledge as such reveals this quantum relativity of perspective. Everything that can be known depends on Maisie's age, upbringing, gender, and angle of vision, all constantly changing as time passes and she becomes increasingly aware of her body and sexuality—literally, as she gets taller and her perspective changes in relation to a rotating cast of vertically static adults. But knowing in *Maisie* also reveals the degree to which knowledge is in a contradictory relationship to not-knowing: the more one knows, in the zero sum game of the novel, the more one recognizes how much is not known and may never be known; the agency of the knowing subject utterly depends on its contingency to the unknown, not as a form of skepticism, but as a recognition that the positive content of knowledge is simply not presently available and may never arrive.

Consider the title of the novel: *What Maisie Knew.* It suggests that we are to be exposed to the contents of the protagonist's knowledge, but the title poses a series of quandaries different from those that might have arisen had the title been *What Maisie Found Out,* which appears to be the working title for many of the novel's readers, as if it were a detective story. The title *What Maisie Knew* is cast in the past tense, and gives rise to the possibility that this may be a story of repression and forgetting as much as it is of acquiring knowledge. Maisie may have forgotten what she once knew; perhaps what she once knew as part of a traumatic childhood will be transformed into false memories as she moves into the adulthood portended at the end of the novel. The statement of the title generates nothing but questions: Did Maisie know more or less? Did she know everything she could have known, or is there either more that she could have known but didn't, or more that she could not possibly have known but that we do, or could have, or will know, if we read the novel? In the tense of our reading of the novel (that of the future perfect) what is it that Maisie *will have known* when she departs on the ship from Boulogne-Sur-Mer to recross the English Channel, now, in effect, orphaned and with the indomitable Mrs. Wix in tow, "condemned," as James devilishly puts it, "to know more and more," which raises the further question, "how could it logically stop before she should know Most?"[9] James capitalizes the *M* of the "most" in that question, as if it were some delimited totality—some "all" of the knowable—to which Masie might, would, or could have access if, based on what she has known in the past, her agency as knowing subject could be extended into an unmarked, unnarrated future. And what is the "more" and "Most" in play here: Reality with a big *R*? Adult sexuality? The perfidy of human nature? Once the discovery has been made that the good parent, or good spouse, or good friend is a paper tiger and that the "real" of Reality is a tissue of fabrications full of holes, then one has already breached the "Most" of the knowable in Jamesian terms. In its ironic maliciousness, Maisie's condemnation to the knowledge of the totality of an unknown something in the future and our ignorance of what that might be (the reader become John Marcher) is indicative of a deep anxiety—James's anxiety—about the extent to which the known only becomes available in its adjacency to the overwhelming unknown in the distance.[10]

Throughout his career, James took seriously the responsibility of representing "the human scene" in its multidimensionality as a display of tiled, overlapping optical performances. But the arc of that career can be traced as a growing recognition, especially in the late fiction and the prefaces, that the field of vision is not merely delimited by what it cannot possibly include (the unknown, the unknowable as-yet-to-be-known), but is only visible, like an aberration of starlight, by means of an angled gaze more directly aimed at the darkness all around it. We have seen how, in the preface to *Roderick Hudson*, James's attractions to the "lure of detail," as well as the accompanying retrospective "terror" stemming from the inability to fully represent the overwhelming totality of "the vast expanse of that surface" of the visible, reveals the degree to which the very concept of the optic surface, the human scene, relies upon a good many black holes, the empty perforations not of the in- but of the non-visible.[11] We might consider this the terror brought about by what James knew, not at the time of the writing of *Roderick Hudson*, but at the time he is looking in the rear view mirror after writing *Maisie*, "The Beast in the Jungle," "The Turn of the Screw," *The Wings of the Dove*, *The Golden Bowl*—these dramatizations of dangerous, abject knowledge that characterize late James.

What is so terrifying about this recognition of the incapacity to represent a totality? Žižek suggests in a reading of *The Wings of the Dove* that the effect of such knowledge—which depends entirely upon what is not known, or upon what can only be known through another who serves as the guarantor of one's self-knowledge—becomes a form of embarrassment that reveals the disabling codependency of intersubjective knowledge, rather than the comprehensive possibilities of its happier versions. For Žižek, the very grammar of *Wings*—its employment of "appositive deixis," or the placement of the pronoun coming before the subject "which follows in apposition" in such phrases as "She waited, Kate Croy, for her father to come in"—introduces a "minimal" gap between subject and qualification that reveals the degree to which subjectivity, all by itself, is "not a thing to which attributes are attached and which undergoes changes—it is a kind of empty container, a space in which things can be located."[12] In the domain of epistemology where the interaction between subjects produces intersubjective knowledge, "the whole psychic economy of a situation changes radically" only when two or more subjects become aware of what the others know or don't know (or, in more Jamesian fashion, they find out that others knew all along what they didn't know). The result is a negation of agency: "for Densher, marrying Kate while accepting money from the dead Milly became impossible the moment he learns that Milly knew about his and Kate's plot."[13] Here as elsewhere in late James, the positivity of agency relies entirely on an erratic contestation between knowing and not-knowing: had Kate and Densher remained in ignorance of Milly's knowledge of their scheme (or had Milly, impossibly, remained in ignorance of it) then the marriage plot would have been completed with the inheritance; had Kate and Densher, knowing of Milly's knowledge, agreed to reject the bequest in ignorance of its amount, the marriage plot would have been completed without the inheritance. But the marriage plot of the novel falters on a disparity of knowledges: everyone has either known too much or too little at different points in time, and it is this relativistic knowledge—the antinomy of being ignorant of what is already known—that both kills the marriage and kills Milly. To return to the preface to *Roderick Hudson*, James, looking back at the end of his career to his second novel, exhibits an existential awareness of the fragility of authorial subjectivity and agency that produces terror. These epistemological discomforts are concomitant with acts of seeing and knowing as he reflects on the degree to which the authoring of the positive image (the raised texture of the embroidery) utterly depends upon the negative, the weave of unfilled holes that constitute for James the unrepresented, thus the unknown. The fact that both the knowable and the unknown rests upon the selecting (authorial) subject, which in turn is constituted solely by those shots in the dark, is, for him, cause for anxiety.

I shall discuss more fully in chapter 5 how James's conflation of visuality with epistemology informs his late fiction; for now, we can observe that friction and slippage generated by the contact between the seen and the known worries James through the prefaces, and places him at one end of the arc that I will trace to Haneke's contemporary concerns with mediation and surveillance in *Caché*. In the preface to *The Golden Bowl*, James provides another interesting figure that, for Rebecca Walkowitz, reveals the tendency in late James to build his work "on the foundation of absent narrative," envisioning "his task as the evocation of insufficient representation."[14] Here, James seems concerned to mark representational insufficiency by informing his readers that there are "ever so many more of the shining silver fish afloat in the deep sea of one's endeavor than the net of wide casting could pretend to gather in."[15] This slightly regretful figure comes at the end of a long reflection on the act of revision—to be sure, the secondary revision James was undertaking in writing the Prefaces in the first place. Those "shining silver fish"? The only other place James uses the word "silver" in this preface to a novel about golden bowls occurs when he reflects on the author's "active sense of life":

> The "taste" of the poet is, at bottom and so far as the poet in him prevails over everything else, his active sense of life: in accordance with which truth to keep one's hand on it is to hold the silver clue to the whole labyrinth of his consciousness. He feels this himself, good man—he recognizes an attached importance—whenever he feels that consciousness bristle with the notes, as I have called them, of consenting re-perusal; as has again and again publicly befallen him, to our no small edification, on occasions within recent view.[16]

While James seems to believe that there is a single, silver clue to the "labyrinth" of one's own consciousness—that of the watcher at one of many disparate and detached windows opening out onto the "show" of reality—he also recognizes that consciousness (transposed into a "sea") contains far more silver entities (fish, clues, signs) than can ever be incorporated into poetic vision. In the novel that this reflection references, perhaps the nonnegotiable antinomy between the singularity of consciousness and the utter indeterminacy of what consciousness apprehends is represented for James in the shattering of the novel's central, and centralizing symbol, the golden bowl. The image of the author casting nets into the sea of his own consciousness in order to capture the silver clues that stand metonymically for its impossibly complex totality is, as Walkowitz suggests, a trope of modernist insufficiency: the relation between surface and depth is one of opacity; consciousness is conceived as an occluded repository of infinite content and significances or clues that can only be "netted" randomly, contingently; the Christological reference ("I will make you a fisher of men") suggests that for James the work of the artistic consciousness is hermeneutically redemptive ("I will make you a fisher of clues").[17]

This figuration of the oceanic deeps of consciousness, once more, draws a contradictory relation between seeing and knowing that, in effect, provides the author with a mission: to discern the flashes of his own insight that illuminate the extent of the totality that remains in darkness. This figure seems at first glance in startling contrast to simulative senses of visuality such as that of Frederic Jameson's, who observes in Andy Warhol's photography a "new depthlessness" in "the external and colored surface of things—debased and contaminated in advance by their assimilation to glossy advertising images—[which] has been stripped away to reveal the deathly black-and-white substratum of the photographic image which subtends them."[18] Jameson's contemporaneity in relation to James's modernism in this formulation appears to be the relation of the unrepressed to the repressed, the totally visible to the absent or hidden, the indifferent to a difference built on the hermeneutic fantasy of depth and secrecy.[19] Yet I wish to suggest that there is the inception of an antinomy linking visuality to knowledge in James's figures of consciousness that mark his pre-cinematic anxieties and investments, which more are fully realized in such contemporary metafilms as *Caché*, *Memento* (2000), *Mulholland Drive* (2001) and *Adaptation* (2002) that variously engage in the representation and critique of the manifestations of Jamesonian totality or depthlessness.

The possibility of total exposure—the suggestion that there is a "whole" to and for the visible—is premised on the paradox of this totality's partial visibility and parceling, its "netting," its filming. Implicitly, James is already on to one of the resident contradictions of Jameson's notion of visuality: that the more available the totality of reality becomes to visualization (the example comes to mind of London as a city with so many surveillance cameras that everything and everyone who passes through the city center is continuously being recorded) the less transparent it is. In thinking about the possibility of an unrepressed, virtual totality—that is, materially, a vast plain of indifferent, thoroughly contingent objects or sites to which we have 24/7 access and the technical capacity that allows all of it to be available to continuous exposure—we come up against, as Bazin recognized early on, the intransigent materiality of the medium itself. For the (im)possibility of this totality comes to us by means of the anachronistically modern (and Jamesian) device of the window, aka the browser, the lens, the network, the perusal of the gaze indicative of the bristling consciousness of a thoroughly modern subjectivity.

Surveillance is, in part, the subject of *Caché*, a film that in its very title promises to chart the ratio between exposure and concealment. *Caché* portrays the specter of bourgeois, white, colonialist guilt haunting Europe. It does so via the exposure of protagonist Georges Laurent's guilty childhood past, which he is forced to confront when the first of a series of surveillance tapes arrive on his doorstep showing the entrance to his

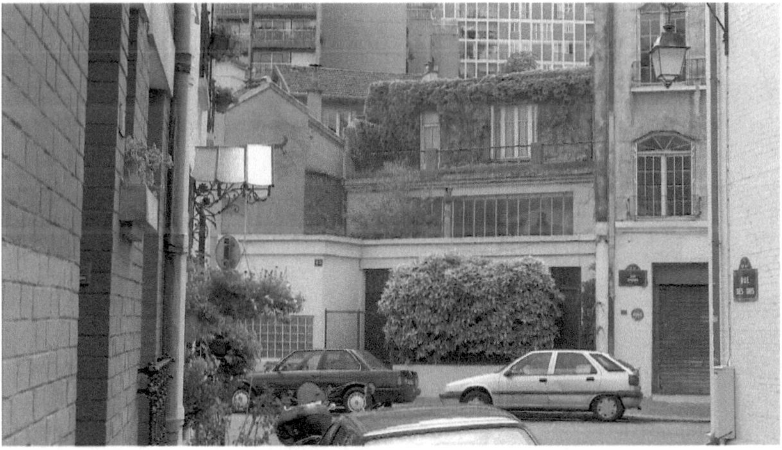

Figure 3.1. Surveillance of the Laurents' apartment in *Caché*. *Caché*, Les films de losange, 2005. Frame capture courtesy of Joshua Yumibe.

apartment building over several hours. We see this tape running in the opening sequence of the film as the credits unroll, but on first viewing it appears to be the film itself until a slight distortion reveals that what we are actually seeing is the digital surveillance tape that Georges and his wife, Anne, are watching on their high-def TV screen.

Fast-forwarding through several hours of the tape, the Laurents view the exterior of their apartment, an occasional pedestrian or passing car, and Georges leaving the apartment for work as a TV cultural talk show host. This is the first of several long shots in the film that puts into question the medium we are watching—one only resolved in the opening shot by virtue of the visual noise induced by fast-forwarding that makes it clear we are watching a videotape within a film. In fact, *Caché* is "Haneke's first use of high-definition video cameras which allow him to set up a narrative device that will mix the images from the videotapes with the images of Georges' 'life.' "[20] This narrative device ensures that throughout the film we are often uncertain about the medium we are watching, leading to both affective indeterminacy and temporal confusion. Corresponding to cinematic temporality evident in the pastiche of the *Kill Bill* films that foments questions about the relationship between time and knowledge, the rewinds and fast forwards of *Caché*'s establishing shot (as the husband, of course, seizes the remote control from his wife) generates ambiguity about the tense of the film (unfolding present? historical past? present or past as being-recorded, or present or past as being-remembered?) and, thus, the valences of any given sequence. Who is being watched, and why? Is their status that of guilty subjects, or innocents being stalked? Are the images that they are compelled to observe a cause, or an effect? And is the compulsion to watch, rewind, and watch again, for either Georges or Anne, who initially appear at least to know not what the tape is or why it has come to them, in the service of revelation or disavowal?

Narratively, acknowledgement and disavowal made visible are at the heart of *Caché*, which, fundamentally, is a film about filming, the medium of film, and the visual media that contest for primacy with film in the digital age. As he investigates the unknown source of the tapes which begin to affect ever-widening dimensions of his personal and professional life, Georges is led to Majid, an Algerian orphan who Georges's parents considered adopting after Majid's parents were killed in the October 17, 1961 massacre of more than 200 Algerians by the French police—an attack on peaceful marchers orchestrated by then Paris Chief of Police Maurice Papon, who twenty years later was revealed to be a Nazi collaborator during the Vichy regime.[21] Not wanting to share his boyhood bedroom or his existence with Majid, we discover in confessional memories apparently wrenched out of him as the result of his adult encounter with Majid, who is now aged beyond his years and living a marginal life in the *banlieues*, that boy Georges has orchestrated Majid's exile to an orphanage by convincing his parents that Majid is mentally unstable and potentially violent. The source of the surveillance tapes and the gory, childlike drawings that accompany them is never made clear in the film: Majid himself? Majid's son, a dispossessed young man only a few years older than Georges's own son, Pierrot? Some third party (perhaps the party of the political unconscious) out to terrorize and expose Georges? What is clear is that Georges's personal story and the forced recovery of a guilty past is made homologous to the French national narrative and the repressed, collective guilt to be borne by the white, European subject whose comforts have been purchased at the costs of racism and genocide. More broadly, as the film makes quite apparent in scenes where news reports on the torture of Iraqis are playing on the television while Georges and Anne discuss their personal dilemmas, the guilt is that of the ongoing present—that of American imperialism and the West writ large.

What is most interesting about *Caché* is not these painfully obvious sutures of the personal to the political, but the fact that the exposure of the repressed past occurs through a mixture and mixing up of mediums that cannot be representationally or ontologically assorted according to their capacity either to metonymically signify the totality of historical reality or its framing as a mode of repression that conceals the dirty secret of historical erasure. As Maurice Blanchot has written, "the stratagem of the secret is either to show itself, to make itself so visible that it isn't seen (to disappear, that is, as a secret), or to hint that the secret is only secret where there is no secret, or no appearance of the secret."[22] The nature of the secret in this view sounds remarkably like the status of the object in Žižek's discussion of Antonioni's metacinematic experiment *Blow-Up*, where, in the closing scene of the film, which features people playing tennis without a ball, we see not a game played "without an object" or "set in motion by a central absence," but rather a game that displays "the object directly, allowing it to make visible its own indifferent and arbitrary character."[23] In *Caché*, the twinned secrets of Georges's guilty childhood and France's guilty Nazi/colonial past are positioned as both utterly available for representation, and at the same time, not secrets at all, both intimately and arbitrarily connected. The medium for the transmission of the contemporary secret is, of course, the surveillance camera, which offers the post-Jamesian fantasy of being able to capture everything that goes on without the intervention of a human operator. To be sure, a single surveillance camera cannot take in the totality of the real, but the device itself, as the efficacious embodiment of mechanical reproduction, infinitely multiplied, promises the possibility of total representation. At the same time, the individual camera—the one deployed at several sites in the film (or is it several cameras deployed at several sites?) enables the representation of the total surface that it surveys within its narrow range along with the assumption that this surface will yield up the entirely visible secrets and identities of the subjects traversing it.

In *Caché*, the identity of he, she, or it who has begun the surveillance of the exterior of the Laurents' flat, or who has placed the same or different cameras across the street from Pierrot's school or inside Majid's tenement apartment, remains a secret. By implication, especially when one considers the threads that connect Georges's childhood to the Algerian massacre in Paris, the surveillance arises from the very Hegelian historical totality for which the surveillance camera serves as a local embodiment, thus representing the omniscient drive behind surveillance. *Caché* negotiates this fantasy of the unrepressed real, but only to show a return to the Jamesian frame in the form of a technological ambiguity that invokes the unseen, the invisible, and the unrepresentable as the consequences of perceptual limitation. Here, epistemological ambiguity exists in inverse ratio to the technology of visibility. Throughout the film, it is often unclear whether we are seeing a rewound tape, looking through the lens of a surveillance camera in real time, or looking through a still camera capturing the light bouncing off bodies and buildings from a reenacted past, and it seems like the more we see, the less we know.

This mediational ambiguity signifies the radical indeterminacy underlying the notion of total visibility—an indeterminacy captured both visually and thematically in the closing scene of the film, which bookends the establishing shot as a long take of the exterior of a building. The building is Pierrot's school; as at the beginning, it is apparently an external long shot taken by a positioned, anchored camera. Previous to this final shot, we have witnessed Majid committing suicide by cutting his throat with a straight razor in his apartment where he has summoned Georges to witness the event, following a confrontation in which Georges refuses to take responsibility for Majid's ruined life. The film's final take

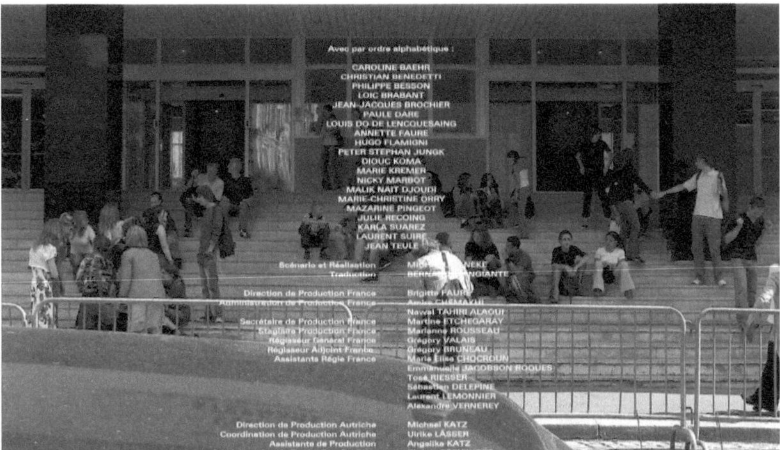

Figure 3.2. School's out as the credits roll in *Caché*. *Caché*, Les films de losange, 2005. Frame capture courtesy of Joshua Yumibe.

offers anything but closure to these scenes of guilt, denial, and their fatal consequences.

Despite the effect of seeing everything that happens in this after-school collectivity within the purview of the camera (the framing of the "show," in Jamesian terms), this surveillance, like all other forms of surveillance in the film, only results in further mysteries. We witness Majid's son conversing with Pierrot, and then moving off camera as Pierrot returns to his group of friends: is Majid's son befriending Pierrot? Is he telling Pierrot that his father is a guilty bourgeois subject (something Pierrot knows already as the thirteen-year-old son of a guilty bourgeois subject)? If the former, does the befriending taking place represent a promise (the sons of the colonizer and the colonized will join as equals) or a threat (the son of the colonized will take his revenge on the son of the colonizer)? And either way, why does Haneke represent this symbolic moment as a metonymical afterthought in the rolling credits? We are still at a loss as to who is continuing to surveil Pierrot or why; perhaps, in this post-pedagogical moment, the film telling us that this is how history is made, via the continued surveillance of subjects for reasons ultimately unknown. These questions, stemming from a Jamesian anxiety about the capacity of the viewer or viewfinder to register all of the seen (James, then, in retrospect, proleptically serving as a camera with a consciousness), remain in circulation in *Caché*'s envisioning of an exposed past. Which is to pose the possibility of a future of total surveillance (video cameras, everywhere) that paradoxically only serves to increase the indeterminacy of the real, even if we were to impossibly frame or capture all of it.

Guilt and innocence mapped onto what can be seen or not seen, what should be seen or what is disavowed, are linked thematically in both *What Maisie Knew* and *Caché* as matters of inheritance and parental pedagogy. The name of Georges's son provides a clue: Pierrot is also the name of the famous clown of French *commedia dell'arte* who pantomimes sadness at his inability to romance his master's daughter.[24] As the inheritor of colonial guilt, Georges's son, in his naming and his contact with Majid's son, might be said to reflect what Paul Gilroy terms "postcolonial melancholia," or the condition of a former empire (in this case, France) that exhibits in its national politics "symptoms that build upon and divert patterns of imperial melancholy"—a "guilt-ridden loathing and depression" that manifests themselves in "xenophobic responses to strangers," largely writ as aliens, immigrants, and racial others.[25] Viewed through the kinds of facile versions of multiculturalism that Gilroy critiques as complicit with the continuance of colonialism, Pierrot's and Majid's afterschool meet might be seen as a joining or equalizing of racial difference that offers a movement beyond the guilty racialized past experienced by their parents. But I think not. Haneke is quite careful to cancel out any easy logic that might lead to this outcome, not only through the high quanta of indeterminacy he brings to mediation, but also narratively in the horrific scene of Majid's suicide, a startling rejection of any historical reconciliations or forms of forgiveness that might accommodate postcolonial guilt or any utopian bridging of racial difference. Regarding social and historical violence, Haneke's vision is as bleak here as it is in the first version of *Funny Games* (1997), where the domestic peace is thoroughly shattered, never to be restored, in the embodiments of the barbaric violence repressed in a "civilized" patriarchy, or in *The White Ribbon* (2009), where fascism continues to have its day beneath the guise of historical and generational change in a German village.

Indeed, in *The White Ribbon*, Haneke locates the transmission of political violence from parents to children, and while James, in *What Maisie Knew*, is more interested in the violent fantasies of an abandoned child then he is in the violence of empire, he does make similar narrative connections as Hanneke in suggesting that the child inherits, in some fashion, the transgressions of the parents. Maisie's knowledge is sexual knowledge; it is adulterous (and adulterated) knowledge that comes in the wake of her parents' prolificacy. What is she to do with it? How is she to grow and live with it? The same questions might be posed to Pierrot, the inheritor of colonial guilt: Once he understands the past, his privilege, his parents' and his nation's complicity, if he ever does, how will he live? What shape will his recognitions take, and will he (Hanneke asks, how can he not?) replicate in some fashion the forms of disavowal upon which his world and its institutions, like the school into which Pierrot finally disappears, are built? Similarly, James envisions Maisie disappearing with her "mentor" Mrs. Wix into the interior of the English homeland, having learned what she has learned, and knowing what she knows, after the culminating experience of a flight to European shores—always, for James, the site of innocence perverted. For both James and Haneke, the problem of visibility, evident in these narrative and cinematic exposés of the extent to which the seen/known is hedged by the unseen/unknown, is addressed authorially in the epistemological quandaries of *What Maisie Knew* and the mediational indeterminacies of *Caché*. These are works in which anxieties about what might be known and the consequences of knowing too much contend with each other in the production of the knowing and, thus, guilty subject.

Chapter 4

Mementos

"The Beast in the Jungle" and *Memento*

In the discussion of temporality and mortality in James and Tarantino that occupies chapter 2, childhood experience is registered as a confrontation between a continuous present and the rupture in that continuum that occurs when death is brought into view. In this chapter, I will consider how modern temporality and its discontents in the work of memory are negotiated between a story about an obsessive relation to the future and a film about an equally obsessive relation to the past—relations that are, once again, overseen by voyeuristic identities. Both James's "The Beast in the Jungle" and Christopher Nolan's film *Memento* are illustrative of James's intense sense of modern temporality as, in Sylviane Agacinski's elegant phrase, "the endless interlacing of the irreversible and the repetitive."[1] And in both the story and the film—the latter, in many ways, an uncanny visualization of the temporality of the former—memory is, in effect, the narrative construction of time, or what can be conceived as a highly reflexive narrative projection across the immense gaps opened up by "the endless interlacing of the irreversible and the repetitive" tending toward the mortal future. In reading James in this way, I will rely on the work about temporality and futurity of the post-Hegelian philosophers Giorgio Agamben in *Infancy and History* and Agacinski in *Time Passing: Modernity and Nostalgia*, and Mary Anne Doane's reading of the relation between temporality, death, and the visual image in *The Emergence of Cinematic Time*. My goal is to see how James's narrative is illuminated by examining how cinematic notions of temporality, informed by contemporary, hyperbolic notions of the rush of time and the brevity of memory, are visualized in Nolan's symptomatic film. Both, I will suggest, are millennial narratives that reflect a fear of futurity and a desire to pass the time by killing time.

❧

Something of a cliché itself, modernity is all too often in its formulaic representations associated with amnesia, but having turned the corner on a shell-shocked, amnesiac century and proceeded chaotically down the road of the next one, in retrospect, we seemed besotted—at least in the movies clustered around the new millennium's beginning—with cinematic narratives depicting memory gone wrong.[2] Some examples: films about people who have forgotten they are dead and who think they are still alive (*The Others*, 2001) or who just remembered once more that they are dead (*The Sixth Sense*, 1999); people who forcibly forget to remember and then remember to remember that their first meeting is actually their second (*Eternal Sunshine of the Spotless Mind*, 2004); people whose memory of their supposedly dead children is diagnosed as paramnesia, or the projection of false memory, when actually their children have been abducted by aliens and the process of erasing their memories somehow bungled by the superior beings conducting experiments on human memory (*The Forgotten*, 2004); and a man whose short-term memory is so defective that the recent past must exist as a pastiche of corporeal inscriptions in a series of takes that move forwards through time as the *récit* of the film moves backwards (*Memento*, 2000). Perhaps these films and others like them, screened for a public experiencing amplified fears of the unknown as the millennium moved from the rear view mirror to the road ahead, reflect a nostalgic fantasy for a more stable time when memory seemed more important, more hooked into temporality unfolding in some perceptible fashion that related past, present, and future. That is, a time "before" the advancement of the digital age to the point where the threat of a global computer virus would spell the end of the world, or "before" 9/11, even if that event could have only been anticipated before it happened in the fabulistic reverse-engineering of retrospect. But nostalgia and retrospect constructed in this manner are based upon false memories rendered palpable, as Agacinski suggests, by a sense of being displaced from "the continuity of history," or history viewed as a "comprehensive movement" toward a "unique direction."[3] Among other things, the advent of the twenty-first century seems to mark a dividing line between this "before" and "after"—one confirmed by actual events, and one that posits a before that has little to do with the ruptures and displacements of the time in which it is located.

If we look to the beginning of a century (the twentieth) that we can't seem to put behind us, where one might expect to locate some or the origins of those tendencies that reach full bloom in the contemporary portrayals of the rupture between time and memory, we find Freud, in *The Psychopathology of Everyday Life* (1901), talking about memory as the quanta of the quotidian, and we find Henry James, in "The Beast in the Jungle" (1903), portraying a man obsessed with manufacturing the memory of a future he cannot quite project. In the introductory essay on the forgetting of proper names, Freud posited that developing a theory of repression was going to allow him, preliminarily, to "add a *motive* to the factors that have been recognized all along as being able to bring about the forgetting of a name; and in addition . . . [to elucidate] . . . the mechanism of false recollection (paramnesia)."[4] Freud was envisioning a process by which we willfully forget something in the past in order to unwillingly remember something else that enables and screens this first forgetting. At the same moment, James was creating a protagonist in "The Beast in the Jungle" who enacts a kind of reverse paramnesia by figuring forth a false future in believing himself "kept for something rare and strange, possibly prodigious and terrible" that will occur at some indeterminable point in time.[5] And at the end of the century in which James expired, putatively moving into something beyond the modern, beyond the postmodern, beyond analog and beyond repression, into translucent, global, digital knowledge networks and a world of globally challenged Americans, we have these affect-ridden cinematic portrayals of memory gone awry in time, all suggesting that we have forgotten something important along the way.

Bookending the century, both James and Nolan crucially reflect on the stakes involved in forging the relation between memory-making and temporality: the construction of a future in the face of the modern experience of time, characterized by Agamben as an "elusive flow of instants," "no more than a simple succession of *now* in terms of before and after."[6] Under this formulation, the work of memory is not to recollect or recover a past that has only existed, when it was present, as an elusive flow of instants; rather, for James's Marcher, obsessing about a future that never comes to pass, and for *Memento*'s paramnesiac subject, beset by signs of a past that block any knowledge or vision of a future to come, memory is the work of merely overseeing the passing of time. Yet this "merely" has the potential to constitute—as it does for James and as it does not for Nolan—the depth of the subject before death.

❧

It is quite remarkable what one finds, Google search engine fired up to ascertain whether plagiarism has taken place while adventuring into the jungles of the internet with a query containing the keywords "Henry James future." On the site known as the "Henry James Discussion Desk," clearly a blog for students in search of paper topics, one finds the following comment from one "Mary J. Speed":

> I don't see as much [homosexuality] in John Marcher as I see a man who never grows up. That is the Beast—adulthood. Some people are not naturally able to study and predict adult life as are others, and Marcher is one of these. About the time he figures anything out, his golden chance has [s]ped with the ping of May Bartram. Some people say Pisces only grow up around age 40. Some say that Geminis never grow up and neither do Virgos. My guess, with all the emotional introspection that Marcher does, is that he depicts a Pisces. Pisces see adulthood all around them but never have a clue about how to organize emotionally to it themselves. This explains the constant "bethought himself"-ing that Marcher does. Only people who do not know [how to grow up] spend their time reminiscing about the present! Marcher does so [throughout] the whole story. Even as he falls on May's tomb, he is in the present. The man never has any clue about the future, but constantly imagines what it hold[s]—never a clue about what adulthood is really about.[7]

What might appear on the surface to be a naïve and largely irrelevant commentary, in fact, identifies matters of temporality, maturation, and sexuality as at the heart of James's turn-of-the-century story. Or rather, it brings them together only to sequester them. As Eric Savoy has shown, building upon Sedgwick's infamous reading of "the beast in the closet," sexuality and the rhetoric of temporality are inextricably bound together in

James fiction, yet here, the reader wishes to insist that the story is about one by not being about the other.[8] In this way, she uncannily repeats Marcher's fundamental gesture in "The Beast in the Jungle," which is to construct the future as a formal rhetorical category that can be partitioned off from other, equally formalized temporal categories, effectively preventing them from bleeding into the "mess" of identity and experience.

As many have remarked, Marcher is paranoid, but the particular form Marcher's paranoia takes in relation to the fabrication of the future is to perceive it, as I have remarked in another context, as a *punctum caecum*, a temporal blind spot disconnected from past and present, yet overdetermined with projections about what, unseen, is to come—projections issuing solely from a paranoid identity in the form of a disavowal of temporality per se in the manufacture of a figure that disguises such denial.[9] Thus Marcher, encountering an acquaintance, May Bartram, at the forebodingly named estate of Weatherend, and anxious that this re-encounter with an individual from a forgotten past will be his last, struggles to reverse the projected abortive future of their relationship and is depicted as "almost reaching out in imagination—as against time—for something that would do, and saying to himself that if it didn't come this sketch of a fresh start would show for quite awkwardly bungled."[10] It is May, not Marcher, who saves the moment (and their future together), by reversing his amnesia about confessing to her—and her alone—the knowledge of the selective fate that he believes awaits him during their first encounter in Naples. This double-reversal reveals Marcher's characteristic relation to temporality as a series of blockages or blinds—obstructions that are removed only by means of the work of some external agency (in this case, May). Through her recollection, she enables a productive relation between Marcher's amnesia and his paranoid projections about a future in which he is at the absolute center, destiny's special case. And indeed, it will require another external agent, Marcher's "neighbor at the other grave"[11] whose suffering Marcher voyeuristically experiences, to propel Marcher toward the consequential future he has "missed" through self-induced amnesia in regards to the past and a mania of projective referentiality in regards to the present. Out of time at May's grave, Marcher perceives the future as a sequestered site that, it turns out, is void of content, and he "the man of his time, *the* man, to whom nothing on earth was to have happened."[12]

Marcher's experience of temporality is one in which disconnected *puncta* saturated with immediacy occur in the field of a present sealed off from an amnesiac past and voided future, where the syntax of intention and agency is cast in the form of "was to have been." For Agamben, this experience is characteristic of modernity as such. As he writes in "Time and History: Critique of the Instant and the Continuum": "The fundamental contradiction of modern man is precisely that he does not yet have an experience of time adequate to his idea of history, and is therefore painfully split between his being-in-time as an elusive flow of instants and his being-in history, understood as the original dimension of man."[13] This split—a form of schizophrenia in Agamben's hands that can only be cured by reinvigorating historical experience with pleasure—comes about because of the disconnection that Marcher symptomatically embodies between temporality as, in Agamben's terms, an "infinite *continuum* of precise fleeting instants" and history as a productive narrative wherein agency is a matter of active recollection transforming the future.[14] In an instance of Jamesian historical irony, May, in her grave—perhaps especially in her grave—still retains the power to enact such transformations as those she initiated Weatherend in compelling Marcher to remember Naples.

Especially in her grave, especially as Marcher gazes upon another man mourning and visually traces May's name inscribed in the headstone:

> The name on the table smote him as the passage of his neighbor had done, and what it said to him, full in the face, was that *she* was what he had missed. . . . So he saw it, as we say, in pale horror, while the pieces fitted and fitted. So *she* had seen it, while he didn't, and so she served at this hour to drive the truth home. It was the truth, vivid and monstrous, that all the while he had waited the wait itself was his portion. This the companion of his vigil had a given moment made out, and she had then offered him the chance to baffle his doom. One's doom, however, was never baffled.[15]

For an epiphany, as James clearly suggests in the loaded, temporizing repetitions of Marcher's "recognitions," this one leaves a lot to be desired. One might view Marcher's recognition of the proper name ironically as akin to those Freud described in the *Psychopathology*—in truth, hardly dramatic or apocalyptic: semantically overdetermined, but seemingly affectively insignificant. It serves Marcher's purpose, of course, to have the awful truth be "monstrous," coming in the form of a ghostly possession (again, agency externalized) as Marcher now construes his history, at its end, in the form of a doomed "hauntology." As Derrida writes in *Spectres of Marx*, we condemn ourselves to history as a form of haunting, a ghosting of our own temporality, "as long as one relies on a general temporality or an historical temporality made up of the successive linking of presents identical to themselves and contemporary with themselves."[16] It is, precisely, this "general temporality" that Marcher inhabits at the end of "The Beast in the Jungle." He occupies it not as a renunciation of everything that has led him to missing the future in light of his recognition of having done so, but as a repetition of those passive-aggressive strategies—astonished truth-facing at the second remove of voyeurism, forgetfulness/remembering that serves the ends of disavowing agency, insistence on interpretive control over the patterns of narrative and history while affecting submission to them—that he has deployed throughout his career as the man to whom nothing was to have happened. At May's grave, he is "in the moment," past and future now fully apportioned, putatively face to face with himself, confronting the truth and the real work of mourning, prosopopeiacally putting a face on a future that has been faceless (and which, a void, remains so). Yet, in the same instant, he engages in an act of disavowal, "instinctively turning, in his hallucination, to avoid it, he flung himself, on his face, on the tomb."[17] Symptomatically, habitually, Marcher repeats himself in the recognition scene. There is no content to his revelation here, merely a dramatic reflex (literally, a turning from the self-determined figure of fate, thus an attempted double-negation of figurality) resulting in the necrophiliac leap upon the tomb. In the end, his face is pressed up against the inscription of May's name, as if, waiting no longer, acting at last, this manic substitution of the literal with the figural were somehow an adequate retort to a life of formulating the future in terms of a singular figure substituted for the "whole" of the real.

There is, of course, something comically staged and managed about Marcher's theatrical final gesture, as if he were performing for some other unseen mourner watching him and trying to work up the right affect for the occasion. Just as an externalized agency, for Marcher, watching and interrogating him, has always existed as the illusory guarantor of his immersion into a history with an indeterminate yet potentially content-rich future, so, in this final moment, this form of agency is redoubled and inverted as Marcher, in effect, becomes both actor and witness—the very invisibility of the other who sees him serving as the authentication of its presence. Here, a kind of perpetual, self-generating voyeurism is at play, the voyeurism that one sees sketched out in those screwball comedies where a detective is watching a detective is watching a detective who is watching a detective around four corners of a building. Thus, the story forges crucial linkages between voyeurism and temporality in portraying Marcher—the anxious, forward-looking man of the hour—as the would-be ordainer of (his) time.

In their conversation at Weatherend, Marcher and May Bartram set in motion the process that will dictate the terms of their relationship until May's death. They agree that they will jointly "watch" for the signs of the "catastrophe" that is to befall Marcher, which is also an agreement that Marcher will be allowed to watch May watching (who, because she retains the faculty of memory, can act as historian):

> "Then how will it appear strange?"
>
> Marcher bethought himself. "It won't be—to *me*."
>
> "To whom then?"
>
> "Well," he replied, smiling at last, "say to you."
>
> "Oh, then, I'm to be present?"
>
> "Why, you *are* present, since you know."
>
> "I see." She turned it over. "But I mean at the catastrophe."
>
> At this, for a minute, their lightness gave way to their gravity, it was as if the long look they exchanged held them together. "It will only depend on yourself—if you will watch with me."
>
> . . . "Do you think me simply out of my mind?" he pursued . . . "Do I merely strike you as a harmless lunatic?"
>
> "No," said May Bartram. "I understand you. I believe you."
>
> "You mean you feel how my obsession—poor old thing!—may correspond to some possible reality."

"To some possible reality."

"Then you *will* watch with me."

"Are you afraid?"

. . . "I don't know. And I should *like* to know," said John Marcher. "You'll tell me yourself whether you think so. If you'll watch with me, you'll see."[18]

This circular conversation describing the pact between Marcher and Bartram is replete with redundancy: the reiteration of "some possible reality"; the formulation, "if you watch you will see," referring to May's presence in the present moment. Rhetorically, the conversation instantiates a linkage between "watching" and "presencing." The redoubled act of observation—Marcher watching May watching for signs in Marcher of some change in personality or physiognomy indicative of his approaching fate—takes place entirely within the present tense. Or, at least, the present tense for Marcher who can only live in the instant; May, on the other hand, must be there for Marcher because she lives, rhetorically, in a continuum. Reflexive voyeurism—watching the watcher being watched—necessarily serves to connect the instant and the continuum which, Agamben tells us, exist as one in the subject who lives in history, but are split up here between two identities. If we regard "The Beast in the Jungle" as symptomatic of a certain form of modern subjectivity, then, as Marcher's anxiety about having May around to see what happens clearly indicates, voyeurism is not only integral to the formation of this identity—it is absolutely necessary, as both constative and performative act, for its survival and its capacity to make a dangerous world intelligible.

The rhetoric of temporality in James's story about the absence of the historical takes place within a number of significant historical contexts. It comes at the turn of a century that was characteristically accompanied by millenarian fantasies and eschatological projections about the end of time. It appears alongside rapid technological developments in photography and optical instrumentation perhaps only matched by the technological revolution coming at the end of the century that was commencing with the story's publication in 1903, for this was the year in which Pierre and Marie Curie won the Nobel Prize for the development of radioactive substances and the initiation of the science of radiology, which enables the observation of the physical interior. Clearly, we might say, James was onto something in delineating the relation between temporality, observation, and identity in "The Beast and the Jungle," and it will be true that, as these technologies develop, modern subjectivity becomes increasingly defined as something observable in increasingly minute and instantaneous detail. James's critical question in "The Beast in the Jungle" is what does the future hold for such a subject; or, more precisely, what does the subject hold for the future, how does the subject hold onto it?

❧

> He was, we must not forget, almost incapable of general, platonic ideas. It was not only difficult for him to understand that the generic term "dog" embraced so many unlike specimens of different sizes and different forms; he was disturbed by the fact that a dog at three-fourteen (seen in profile) should have the same name as the dog at three-fifteen (seen from the front).
>
> —Borges, "Funes, the Memorious"[19]

Peering nearly a century into that future, we encounter a film completed at the turn of the next century—one that, indeed, portrays a subject whose grasp of the future is synonymous with the forgetting of a past that is divided into "before" and "after" by a brain injury that inflicts upon the film's protagonist the condition of anterograde amnesia. Supposedly (because we are never sure how much of the pre-traumatic past that is the site of permanent memory in his mind is fabricated) Leonard Shelby, an insurance investigator played by an emaciated Guy Pearce, has suffered a head trauma attempting to prevent an intruder in his home from raping and killing his wife. This is the origin of his condition, a type of short-term memory loss defined as:

> Anterograde amnesia . . . a form of amnesia where new events are not transferred to long-term memory, so the sufferer will not be able to remember anything that occurs after the onset of this type of amnesia for more than a few moments. Sufferers from "pure" anterograde amnesia will still be able to remember memories laid down before the onset of anterograde amnesia, but will exist in a transient world where anything

> beyond their immediate attention-span disappears permanently from their consciousness. Someone with anterograde amnesia will generally have good memory for the past, up until the time of the brain injury, but will have extreme difficulty remembering anything that has happened since then. Such a person may not be able to remember what he had for breakfast, what year it is, what he did yesterday, and so on. However, the person's personality, intelligence and judgment may be unaffected. This type of memory disorder is devastating for patients and for their families. Often, individuals with anterograde amnesia have trouble holding a job—not because they are not capable of doing the work, but simply because they have trouble remembering from minute to minute what it is they are supposed to be doing. Currently, there is no known way to repair the brain damage which causes anterograde amnesia. However, the use of memory aids (such as detailed daily schedules) and other methods can help these people cope with their memory disorder. Damage to the hippocampus, fornix, or mammillary bodies can result in anterograde amnesia, suggesting that they are involved in the process of laying down long-term memories.[20]

Obsessed with tracking down and taking his revenge upon his wife's killer despite his condition, which he describes as the inability to "make new memories," Leonard commences an investigation that produces a labyrinth of clues about the killer's identity. He deploys a complex system of "memory aids" or "mementos," to use the film's title, including tattooing messages to himself on his body, constructs elaborate pastiche-like procedural charts, takes Polaroid shots of various players in the mystery, inscribing the photos with reminders about the perceived veracity of the subject, and repeatedly sorts, Columbo-like, through an assemblage of notes, receipts, stray bits of paper, and found objects. It is notable that with Leonard's use of a Polaroid camera, Nolan embeds then-current photographic technology to serve as an inadequate and, often, misleading substitute for Leonard's memory in a cinematic medium that portrays mnemonic disfunction in the visual register.[21] *Memento*'s notoriety resides in its narrative exposition: with the exception of the establishing sequence, which shows Leonard killing a man in frame backward, a couple of days in the life of Leonard Shelby on the trail of the killer is related in the film as a series of time-slices that move in reverse order chronologically but that, within each segment, move narratively forwards in time. These time-slices, filmed in color, are interspersed with segments filmed in black and white (also, collectively, moving forward through time in "normal" narrative chronological order) that depict Leonard in the confessional mode on the phone to a police detective, or perhaps the killer himself playing detective, or perhaps the detective pretending to help Leonard find the killer while using him and his disability to undertake by proxy a series of profitable murders. The black and white sequences tell the story of Sammy Jankis, a man purportedly suffering from anterograde amnesia whom Leonard is investigating in his before-trauma days. It seems clear, as the police detective-cum-serial killer pimp Teddy tells Leonard in the film's climatic sequence, that the story of Sammy Jankis is a screen-memory for Leonard's own complicity in the death of his wife. That this epiphanic revelation comes "backwards" at the beginning of the film's reverse chronology underscores the extent to which past and future are simultaneously fabricated in *Memento*.

It is evident that *Memento* is a film about time and memory that mangles narrative temporalities in such a manner that the relation between past and future is not simply reversed, but made wholly discontinuous, "the endless interlacing of the irreversible and the repetitive" unraveled by the flow of clues, contingencies, and mementos that should add up to the totality of a solution. We recall that a memento is a souvenir, or pleasant reminder of the past, though the word has also been used to suggest a recollection that is simultaneously a warning about the future, along the lines of "those who forget the past are condemned to repeat it." Thus, a memento is a mnemonic device or fetish that links past and future, but one that in historic usage derived from the ecclesiastical traditions of Catholicism, where "memento" refers to two prayers in the Canon of the Mass that commemorate, respectively, the living and the dead. From this usage derives, as well, the notion of a "memento mori," an image or icon popular in the late Middle Ages that caused one to reflect upon one's own mortality; "Memento Mori" is also the title of the short story by Jonathan Nolan upon which his brother's film is based. More recently, the word "memento" has been morphed by the evolutionary biologist Richard Dawkins into "meme," that is, a kind of psuedo-genetic memory unit that can be transmitted between individuals in the same way as viruses and between generations in the same way as DNA—a notion that, whatever its valences, has been the basis for any number of New Age theories, ranging from fundamentalist Christian to Wiccan, about controlling our future and managing our own evolution.[22] While seemingly irrelevant, the curtailing of memento into meme is pertinent to Nolan's film about memory loss and paramnesia in the post-Reagan age where the codependencies of historical amnesia and fantasies of historical transparency abound. The fantasy of a kind of cultural memory gene that survives across individuals and generations and that could authenticate our collective long-term memory is thoroughly dispatched in *Memento*, where the fabrication of the past occurs *a posteriori* to the recollection of a present, a process that takes place precisely by means of that projection after the fact.

What *Memento* does, in other terms, through jump cuts, flashbacks, and the deployment of a palette alternating between color and black and white, is to represent sheer contingency as fatality. In this regard, *Memento* is one of the most "edited" films imaginable as it attempts to simulate the temporality of brain dysfunction, leading to numerous controversies and discussions about the arrangement of the film's time, plot, and structure.[23] Navigating contingencies that have no future in his memory, Leonard is, in effect, Marcher's opposite, as Marcher produces a future where, in retrospect, nothing is contingent because nothing has been experienced in the past as signifying that future. Underlying this formulation of Marcher's recognition is a theory of the event in time, which exists in its full potential as irrelevant and unrelated to destiny until and unless it is recollected as part of pattern of meaningful historical experience. Leonard Shelby, in effect, reverses the process of "recollection" portrayed in "The Beast in the Jungle," as what he "remembers" of the past takes place after a future that has already occurred in the film's opening sequence. The effect can be reproduced in James if we imagine the story opening with the scene of Marcher at May's grave, the remainder of the narrative given over to Marcher's piecing together all of those moments from the past that provided the ignored clues to May as his "good" destiny, each memory-sequence recalled in reverse time. In fact, it is possible to experience "The Beast in the Jungle" in this manner, but only in a recursive reading of the narrative undertaken by those attempting to build interpretive models that would explain what happened to Marcher, how he could have so badly missed his fate, how his future could have come to serve as the replacement for his past—in short, the work of the critic. From this perspective, the obverse relation between *Memento* and "The Beast in the Jungle" could be seen (in the case of the former) as the story of a reader without a text (memory) and (in the case of the latter) the story of a text without a reader, until it is too late.

From one perspective, *Memento* is nothing but a pastiche of images, shots, and angles depicting a protagonist taking notes, tattooing himself, sorting through evidence; thus, it foregrounds its own status as a filmic assemblage of narrative contingencies. In so doing, it poses a question about whether it matters or not if a specific, legitimated narrative emerges out of the assemblage that establishes a relation between story and truth, as long as one can act upon some set of derived significances, some version of "what happened" that makes sense and allows one to relate past to future and contingency to fate. Burt, the manager of the motel at which Leonard is staying (and who has tricked Leonard by renting and charging him for two different rooms because, of course, Leonard can't remember that he's even rented a motel room in the first place for more than fifteen minutes), responds to Leonard's description of his condition with the following: "That must suck . . . All backwards . . . Well, like . . . you gotta pretty good idea of what you're gonna do next, but no idea what you just did. (Chuckles). I'm the exact opposite."[24] Burt suggests that the normative *modus operandi* is for the individual to remember the past perfectly well, but to be clueless as to how to act in the future. In this view, action is premised upon a knowledge or recognition of the past leading toward the opacity of the future, which clarifies slowly as "what you just did" accretes and merges with "what you want to do next," the latter remaining a mystery until an action is completed and remembered, thus effectually providing a past to a future experienced as an opening onto the present.

The sharp difference between Burt's perspective and Leonard's, who must temporize according to the constraints of his condition, is revealed as he discusses the rationale for vengeance in the face of amnesia with Natalie, who, like Teddy, may be using Leonard as a proxy for her own revenge plot:

> NATALIE: But even if you get your revenge, you won't remember it. You won't even know it's happened.
>
> LEONARD (annoyed): So I'll take a picture, get a tattoo. (Calms). The world doesn't just disappear when you close your eyes, does it? My actions still have meaning, even when I can't remember then. My wife deserves vengeance, and it doesn't make any difference whether I know about it.[25]

For Leonard, living in a world that is all contingency where the future is unrelated to the recent past as experienced because that past is being continuously erased, the project of the future is entirely unrelated and irrelevant to what one remembers doing: it is not a mystery to be solved by remembering the past, but a set of non-events marked by representations of the contingencies that have led up to it. Here, contingency takes over event as it is transformed from the quanta that is either significant or irrelevant depending upon what remembered experience holds for the future, into the "all" of event itself. Leonard's plight is that he must make do with the substitution of contingency for memory and event as the base matter for the construction of a relation to time and death. We might view this as the guiltless realm of pure seriality, that reality inhabited by Borges's Funes, who cannot extract the general from the particular.

Yet, appositely, contingency per se is tested in *Memento* as it is whittled down to its quiddity as an isolatable element in the follow of time, a disconnected event-bit reflexively fabricated within the terms of the cinematic decomposition of its own medium that requires an obsessive exertion of will to force it into a temporal narrative order of any kind. The film's double-reflection on contingency and composition is consistent with what Doane considers to be primary to the representation of the modern event:

> Because a fascination with contingency raises the specter of pure loss, the possibility of the complete obliteration of the passing moment, the degradation of meaning [a possibility, we might observe, that is brought to fruition in *Memento*], it also elicits a desire for its opposite—the possibility of structure. Jean-François Lyotard claims that modernity is "a way of shaping a sequence of moments in such a way that it accepts a high rate of contingency." In this definition, contingency coexists happily with the process of "shaping." In the same way, the concept of the *event* is on the cusp between contingency and structure.[26]

Doane locates the more-or-less happy coexistence of contingency and structure at the beginnings of modern film; by the time of *Memento*, the resistance of contingency, in its particulate form, to the structurations of memory is quite evident as the product of Leonard's condition.

In a crucial scene of the film, Leonard investigates the tattoos on his body and photographs and charts on the wall of hotel room for clues to the identity of his wife's murderer. He has forgotten, of course, the contents of the photographs, as well as the fact that he shot and labeled them, or that he has inscribed many of the tattoos he reads as if for the first time. The shot and action directions of the shooting script portray Leonard's investigative technique:

> Leonard inspects the photos. Some are buildings, some are people. All have the HANDWRITTEN NOTES on the broad white strip underneath the image.
>
> Leonard gets Polaroids out of his pocket. The first one is of the Discount Inn. He STICKS it onto an already-squashed lump of blue tack at the end of an ARROW drawn from a location on the outskirts of town. . . .
>
> Leonard hangs up, thinking. He looks at the writing on the back of his hand, then pulls back his sleeve to reveal the words:
>
> "THE FACTS:"
>
> Leonard removes his jacket, then starts pulling off his shirt.
>
> He has WRITING TATTOOED ALL OVER HIS CHEST, STOMACH AND ARMS, MESSAGES in different styles of writing, some CRUDE, some ELABORATE. The messages run in all directions, some UPSIDE-DOWN, some BACKWARDS. Leonard examines his tattoos, methodically. From Leonard's POV, the most striking is an upside-down tattoo on his BELLY which says:
>
> "PHOTOGRAPH: HOUSE, CAR, FRIEND, FOE"
>
> On one FOREARM, it says:
>
> "THE FACTS
>
> FACT 1. MALE
>
> FACT 2. WHITE"

On the other FOREARM:

"FACT 3. FIRST NAME: JOHN OR JAMES

FACT 4. LAST NAME: G-------"

Leonard pulls down his trousers. On his right THIGH, crudely-lettered:

"FACT 5. DRUG DEALER"

And immediately below this, in elegant, neat lettering:

"FACT 6. CAR LICENSE NUMBER: SG13 7IU"

Leonard takes out the REGISTRATION DOCUMENT and examines it. Holding the photo of Teddy and the registration document, Leonard checks off his TATTOOED FACTS;

(under his breath)

White . . . male. First name . . . John. Last name . . . G for Gammell. Drugs. License plate.

(checks document against tattoo on thigh)

SG . . . 13 . . . 7 . . . IU. It's him. It's actually him.

Leonard looks coldly at Teddy's smiling image.

I found you, you fuck.[27]

If John Marcher looked outward to an external world for signs of his fate only to discover it on the verge of the grave's void, Leonard Shelby, in an act of voyeuristic "discipline," as he terms it, looks upon his own body as the site where the structuring of contingency takes place. Regarding his own skin as the only reliable parchment upon which the essential facts and events of the post-traumatic past can be inscribed and connected because he can never lose sight of them while gazing upon himself, he boasts that,

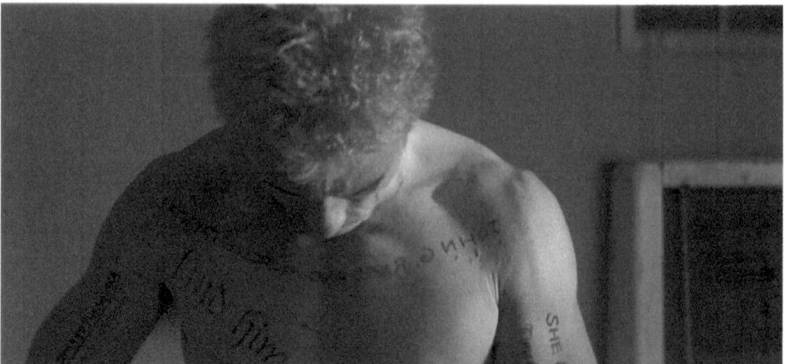

Figure 4.1. Leonard inspecting his tattoos in *Memento*. *Memento*, Newmarket, 2000. Frame capture courtesy of Joshua Yumibe.

unlike Sammy Jankis, he can remember because he has a system. Yet the very elements of his "system" confound him, for the inscriptions on the body are written haphazardly, in every direction and in different fonts, some containing vital information, others wholly irrelevant, though at the time of the inscribing by a professional tattooist or by Leonard himself, using a sewing needle and ink from ballpoint pens, they appeared to be of great importance. Rather than the body being the place where the various placements and hierarchies of the contingent are transformed into a system of information, rather than voyeuristic self-observation being the guarantor of experiential truth and historical continuity, Leonard's corpus is the medium upon which a semi-random assemblage of disparate signs are inscribed in such a way that their separability and contingency are foregrounded, their systematicity disseminated. True, Leonard finds his man using his body as a map, but Teddy is not the one who killed his wife; his existence as a stand-in for the real killer is only an excuse for Leonard to seek continuous vengeance without knowledge or recollection. The only context that Leonard's body provides is that seen in the mirror, a reflected unity only and always viewed in its partiality and reversibility. Thus he constructs the past—that is, he makes new memories—as something that is always, temporally, read backwards, which produces a future, precisely in terms of the film's chronology, as anterior to the past because it is the only future possible for someone who may have an idea about what he wants to do next, but can't remember what he just did.

In the highly self-reflexive, self-conscious narratives of "The Beast and the Jungle" and *Memento*, James and Nolan are fascinated with the foibles of identity assembled across time by means of acts of self-observation that require a partitioning of temporality and a sequestering of contingency. It might be argued that John Marcher and Leonard Shelby are perverse or aberrant examples, the former manufacturing a future that never comes to pass save as a recognition that the content of the future is in the past, the latter manufacturing a past that operates to produce a future of sheer seriality, the irreversible and the repetitive writ large. And yet, could it not be equally argued that they are situated at either ends of a trajectory that Agamben has described as that of modernity in relation to time, "no more than a simple succession of *now* in terms of before and after"? As we have seen, this question poses additional complications for both James and Nolan in terms of their respective mediums, causing/enabling them to perform experiments that challenge their respective medium's limits. For James, this results in a climactic moment built upon an empty anticipatory logic, thus subverting the traditional notions of the relation between cause and effect in the narrative plot. For Nolan, the visual experimentation may be more obvious, as the entire film can be seen as a commentary on the splicing and dicing that occurs in the editing of a film.

What is of greatest interest, to both James and Nolan, is the imaginary relation to temporality that underlies the fantasy of a continuous succession of "nows"—an austere fantasy deployed, for us, in this now, via the idealizations of the cognitive mapping of identity, the lures of the instantaneous and the global, the messy entanglements of putatively "hard" information, affect, and experiential truth. Moreover, this fantasy of immediacy and "present-ness" is wholly consistent with the fantasies of totality and omniscience we have considered elsewhere as limned and undermined by James, Haneke, and Hitchcock, and will see once more in the next chapter's comparison of *The Ambassadors* to *Rear Window*. "How can I heal if I can't feel time?," asks Leonard.[28] How, indeed; but heal from what if the wounding cannot be remembered? In that sense, Marcher, even as the empty iteration of a self-imposed destiny, sees and feels what Leonard cannot: that the gaping wound of the grave before which he stands at the end of "The Beast in the Jungle" signifies the temporal loss that underwrites the contingent relation between life and death. This sad, but oddly seductive and pleasurable recognition, James suggests, enables and reignites the capacity to feel time as a passing away, or passing before, as Leonard would put it, "the facts," which the memento of the body marks in time every day, with each passing hour.

Chapter 5

Experience Machines

The Ambassadors and *Rear Window*

> What words can reproduce the picture these Northern Italian towns project upon a sympathetic retina?
>
> —Henry James, "Travelling Companions"

In the French countryside outside of Paris, Lambert Strether, the central figure of James's 1903 novel, roams a pastoral landscape that seems to be the epitome of a magical accommodation between art, nature, and consciousness such that Strether (via James's capacious use of free indirect discourse) is temporarily assured of a complete and total "fit" between perception and experience:

> For this had been all day at bottom the spell of the picture—that it was essentially more than anything else a scene and a stage, that the very air of the play was in the rustle of the willows and the tone of the sky. The play and the characters had, without his knowing it till now, peopled all his space for him, and it seemed somehow quite happy that they should offer themselves, in the conditions so supplied, with a kind of inevitability. It was as if the conditions made them not only inevitable, but so much more nearly natural and right as that they were at least easier, pleasanter, to put up with. . . . Not a single one of his observations but somehow

> fell into a place in it; not a breath of the cooler evening that wasn't somehow a syllable of the text. The text was simply, when condensed, that in these places such things were, and that if it was in them one elected to move about one had to make one's account with what one lighted on.[1]

One of James's American innocents abroad (innocence qualified—many readers regard him to be a distinctly seriocomic combination of complicitous self-bafflement and obtuseness), Strether has been wandering about the streets of Paris voyeuristically trying to *see* and understand everything in the bewildering assemblage of customs, discourses, histories, and manners that have constituted, up to this climactic point in the novel, his experience of Europe. For nearly three hundred pages, the novel's readers have been exposed to his failure to see and understand, which is identified variously by several parties (Strether himself, other characters, the narrator when he/she/it chooses to hover outside of Strether's head) as a failure of will, imagination, intelligence, and sufficient experience of the world. Now, six months away from his home in stuffy, conventional Woolett, Massachusetts, a place known for its manufacture of undefined widgets, he feels that he is fully immersed in his rich experience abroad—that he is one with it. All the world is a stage in this scene; not a flower is out of place in the countryside landscape; not a typo exists in the text of the internal narrative that translates experience into understanding.[2]

He is wrong, of course, in every way. But the intense pressure that James puts upon this memorable scene reveals yet another iteration of authorial concession transferred, here, into the mind of a protagonist who continuously agonizes about the extent of his understanding and the problem of matching up what he doesn't see with what he does. That concession—that the totality of knowing and seeing anything and everything within any frame of reference exists in direct proportion to the recognized impossibility of doing so—is visible in all of James.[3] As Lynda Zwinger suggests, reading James's "The Art of Fiction" (1894) in which he writes that "experience is never limited and is never complete; it is . . . a kind of huge spider web . . . suspended in the chamber of consciousness and catching every air-borne particle in its tissue," James "declares here his guiding conviction that fiction can be a form of art upon which, like its creator, 'nothing is lost,' . . . all of it can be present, all of it must be included."[4] Yet, as Zwinger goes on to demonstrate and as we have witnessed in the narrative anxieties produced about the knowable in *What Maisie Knew* and Haneke's critique of the panoptic, the proliferation of what can be seen and experienced to every corner of existence serves only to reveal the limitations of what can be seen and the artificiality of the framing of experience. The poignancy of this inverse relation is particularly felt as Strether, blissfully content for the moment in an illusory "total" understanding of land, nature, and people, is about to find out just how distorted his understanding of what is going on around him has been, and to what degree his desire to "see" everything has blinded him to what the "thing" in "everything" is. As Strether thinks it out, the "conditions" that he experiences in the countryside and in a small village where he stops for a solitary meal "were few and simple, scant and humble, but they were *the thing*, as he would have called it . . . 'The' thing was the one that implied the greatest number of other things of the sort he had to tackle, and it was queer of course, but so it was—the implication was complete. Not a single one of his observations but fell into place in it."[5] But this global McGuffin—this conversion of totality of vision and experience into a virtual object—turns out to be no thing, an envelope of experience containing an empty letter.

Leap to Cold War America, and an apartment complex in Manhattan where a man, with a broken leg using technological instruments unavailable to Lambert Strether (at least in their capacities for magnification and resolution), attempts to see everything in the apartments around him. Hitchcock shot *Rear Window* (1954) in its entirety on a single set simulating a Greenwich Village apartment courtyard and composed of layered, windowed cells not unlike those James conceived in the extended "house of fiction" analogy previously considered. Unlike Strether, photojournalist L. B. "Jeff" Jefferies is confined to a wheelchair due to an injury received on the shoot of a car race, but that does not stop him from visually sampling "all of life" as encapsulated by the array of windows facing his own picture window, just as Strether's long walk allows him to scan "everything" to be seen in the French countryside. To be sure, the inhabitants of Jefferies's apartment complex are a limited set of rather unremarkable stereotypes: the well-endowed, flirtatious blonde, the honeymooning couple, the spinster pining for romance, the alcoholic musician (the one gay figure in this heterosexual assortment), the elderly marrieds obsessed with their pet dog, and at the center of it, the shrewish wife and beshrewed husband with a mistress on the side driven to murder. Yet, just as the equally stereotypical French innkeeper Strether encounters stands in for "France" (and everything that might be experienced under that rubric), so too the apartment-dwelling inhabitants of *Rear Window* allegorically figure forth a totality, an "all" of what can be experienced (in this case, love, death, and everything in between) if one just looks closely enough.

Clearly, in both the novel and the film, the role of the mediating consciousness is heightened to the point of absurdity. This is a blind absurdity, readily observed as such by other characters and players, and only deflected by a sudden flash of insight that reveals the ludicrous darkness in which Strether and Jefferies have dwelt, all the while enamored of the illusion that they are seeing and experiencing everything the world has to offer.[6] In France, Strether experiences a higher state of awareness in the wake of the comic orgy of omniscience that has consumed him moments earlier. And it is precisely this elevated condition—antinomically, one of all-seeing blindness—that informs his view of a couple in a boat on a river giving the lie to everything he has thought to be true and authentic about the, seemingly, remarkable Mme. de Vionnet—"the most charming woman in the world" as Maria Gostrey parrots Strether's view of her.[7] In America, the incapacitated photographer is fixated upon the local environment in a heightened state of attention precisely because of this incapacity: his body can't move, but his eyes, aided by camera, binoculars, and telescope, achieve new forms of mobility in the scopic

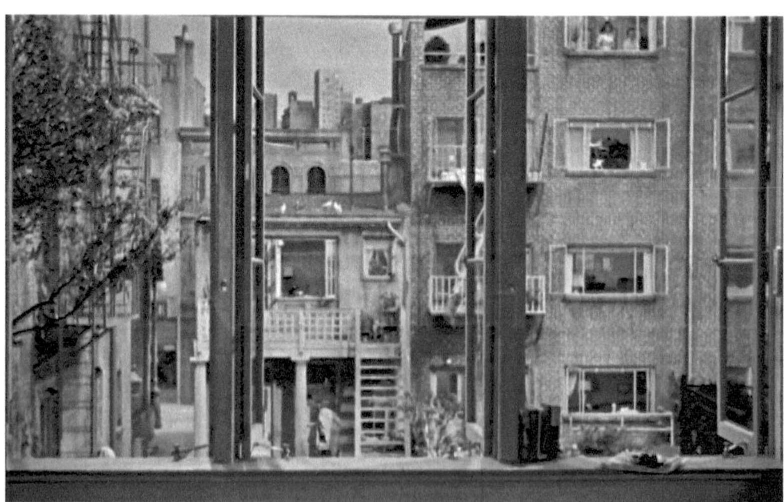

Figure 5.1. The apartment/house of fiction in *Rear Window*. *Rear Window*, Paramount Pictures, 1954. Frame capture courtesy of Joshua Yumibe.

detail of his surroundings. His newly acquired capacities for seeing what has been in front of him all the time enables the conversion of his former vocation of mediating and witnessing big-H historical events into that of a detective who deploys his instruments and his photographic skills—framing, focusing, enlarging—to register the mini-histories taking place all around him and, eventually, to solve a murder.

Yet even with the state-of-the-art equipment of the professional mediator and the wealth of information it provides about the lives of others, Jefferies, brilliantly played by Jimmy Stewart as he alternates between laconic passivity and cranky assertiveness about the truth of what he sees, is hilariously blind to everything about himself. Like *The Ambassadors*, which is largely about Strether's ignorance amidst a wealth of gestures, hints, and messages directed towards him about what is really going on, *Rear Window* is largely about seeing Jefferies seeing everything except what the film is seeing, that is, Jefferies's struggles with his sexual potency and heteronormative identity, his Clouseau-like clumsiness as a detective whose mis-timings and accidents put others in danger, his utter dependence on technology for any truth-bearing occurrences available to consciousness or vision.[8] The anomalies present in Jefferies's role as mediator and detective are nowhere more evident than in the climactic scene where he must pop several flash bulbs in Lars Thorwald's face (played with thuggish abandon by Raymond Burr) in order to stave off the murderer about to strangle the wheelchair-bound man who has "seen" him for the criminal that he is. The flashes of light that save Jefferies's life (and serve as an ironic analogy for the forms of insight offered by Hitchcock's own insight-bearing instrument of choice, the camera) at once illuminate everything and nothing in the white glare that meets the gaze of both detective and murderer, as well as that of the viewer. Tom Cohen reads this scene of illumination as the exposition of "a certain cold real of the murdering cineaste," with Raymond Burr/Thorwald serving as a parodic embodiment of Thor, "Norse god of lightning . . . expunged in Cary Grant's later Empire moniker, Thornhill," a salesman of "costume jewelry" who "cuts up his wife's body, preserves rings," while James Stewart/Jefferies serves as the "photographic tourist" inevitably caught up in one conspiracy or another.[9] In effect, the voyeuristic complicities inherent in the relation between the detective, murderer, and audience are manifested as one dissolves into the other in the white light of the flash, just as the moment of illumination for Strether, as he sees Mme. de Vionnet and Chad Newsome not seeing, and then seeing him seeing them on the river, reveals his self-blinding complicity in the amorous conspiracy.[10]

These episodes are plucked from the unlikely pair of *The Ambassadors* and *Rear Window*, which are both multifarious narratives that implicitly and problematically map the local onto the universal. They both bear remarkable similarities in the need to find an exact match between knowledge and experience, or more precisely, between the "real" and the capacity of mind and body to absorb it *as a totality* through experience technologically enhanced, in the case of Jefferies, or, appositely, peripatetically enhanced, in the case of Strether. The attempted effect is, as Cohen suggests, is one of "naturalizing mimesis" that, in the case of Hitchcock, is foiled by the cinematic medium itself that "technically atomizes" the real, and in the case of James, undone by his pervasive reflexivity about the partiality of perspective (even that of the author forging the multiple perspectives of his characters). These recognitions help to explain the logic behind the revelation of Strether's blindness at the height of a hubristic moment in which he feels that everything fits perfectly into the reality he observes. The same logic is evident in the atomization of the real (surely analogous to the flash of Thor's lightning and that of the hydrogen bomb exploded on the Bikini Atoll in March

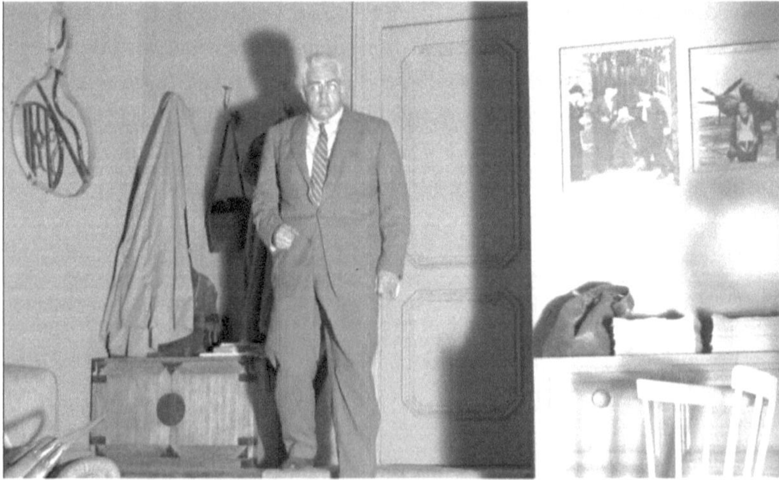

Figure 5.2. Thorwald, caught in the glare of the flash. Note the examples of Jefferies's journalistic photography also caught in the glare as they hang on the wall opposite Jeffries as he "shoots" Thorwald. *Rear Window*, Paramount Pictures, 1954. Frame capture courtesy of Joshua Yumibe.

of the same year as *Rear Window*'s September release) that eclipses the distance between the equally paralyzed Thorwald and Jefferies in the blinding illumination of a flashbulb.

Further, countering this systematic and totalizing view of the available real, rendered as the form of universalism in the array of "types" in *Rear Window* or the staged perfection of "all" of nature in *The Ambassadors*, is the fact that experience, as registered in these narratives, is accidental and partial: revelation is thus, of necessity, thoroughly contingent, an inevitability among multiple inevitabilities whose fatality has been robbed of its agency. Perhaps this is true of any narrative event, but James's narrative reflexivity and Hitchcock's cinematic reflexivity place a unique pressure upon the presumed destinal linkage between reality and experience. In *The Ambassadors*, James is not only setting Strether up for a fall as the consequence of his meanderings in the French countryside. He is quite clearly theatricalizing Strether's itinerary in a manner that offers a commentary on Strether's way of managing what he sees that is eerily similar to the ways in which James manages the novel: as a series of scripted, staged scenes linked by their contribution to a rising or falling dramatic curve and the development of dramatized identities.[11] A slightly different analogy would suggest that Strether experiences "reality" as a series of still-lives, as if Paris and environs were a metropolitan-sized art gallery in which he moves from room to room (as he literally does from hotel rooms and apartments to the drawing rooms and gardens of his French acquaintances), observing paintings, sculptures, and *tableaux vivants*. "For this had been all day the spell of a picture" foregrounds his reflection in the French countryside; an initial stroll with Maria Gostrey through the streets of Chester—with their "rises and drops, steps up and steps down, queer twists, queer contacts, peeps into homely streets and under the brows of gables" yields insight into "certain images of his inward picture"; the "rose-colored shades and the small table and soft fragrance of the lady" at the restaurant where he and Maria dine becomes "so many touches in he scarcely knew what positive high picture"; in early conversations with Strether, Chad Newsome is described as having "in every way the air of trying to live, reflectively, into the square, bright picture" around which Strether is trying to construct a framework of comprehension; the seasons themselves contribute to the portrait of Strether's ongoing confusion and indecision about what to do next in his mission to return Chad to America: "He had in truth at no moment of his stay been so free to go and come. The early summer brushed the picture over and blurred everything but the near; it made a vast warm fragrant medium in which the elements floated together on the best of terms, in which rewards were immediate and reckonings postponed."[12]

These metanarrational indications of Strether's experiences of Europe, arguably a construction of images and scenes parallel to James's construction of the novel, seem to gather hyperbolic force during Strether's train journey and planned descent at a station "selected almost at random" driven by the "impulse—artless, enough, no doubt" to give the whole day "to that French ruralism, with its cool special green, into which he had hitherto looked only through the little oblong window of the picture-frame."[13] This is a fine example of Jamesian irony in play, for nothing could be less "artless" than the sudden memory of a "little Lambinet" (a nineteenth-century French painter of rural scenes) Strether had dreamed of purchasing in younger days:

> It had been as yet for the most part but a land of fancy for him—the background of fiction, the medium of art, the nursery of letters; practically as distant as Greece, but practically also well-nigh as consecrated. Romance could weave itself, for Strether's sense, out of elements mild enough; and even after what he had, as he felt, lately "been through," he could thrill a little at the chance of seeing something somewhere that would remind him of a certain small Lambinet that had charmed him, long years before, at a Boston dealer's and that he had quite absurdly never forgotten. It had been offered, he remembered, at a price he had been instructed to believe the lowest ever named for a Lambinet, a price he had never felt so poor as on having to recognize, all the same, as beyond a dream of possibility. He had dreamed—had turned and twisted possibilities for an hour: it had been the only adventure of his life in connection with the purchase of a work of art. The adventure, it will be perceived, was modest; but the memory, beyond all reason and by some accident of association, was sweet. The little Lambinet abode with him as the picture he would have bought—the particular production that had made him for the moment overstep the modesty of nature. He was quite aware that if he were to see it again he should perhaps have a drop or a shock, and he never found himself wishing that the wheel of time would turn it up again, just as he had

> seen it in the maroon-colored, sky-lighted inner shrine of Tremont Street. It would be a different thing, however, to see the remembered mixture resolved back into its elements—to assist at the restoration to nature of the whole far-away hour: the dusty day in Boston, the background of the Fitchburg Depot, of the maroon-colored sanctum, the special-green vision, the ridiculous price, the poplars, the willows, the rushes, the river, the sunny silvery sky, the shady woody horizon.[14]

I provide this long excerpt whole and complete because it is one of the most concentrated and economic examples of the ways in which Strether thinks and sees in the novel. His illusory immersion into the "real," artless, natural France is preceded by a series of paradigmatic conceptualizations of his experience of Paris/France/Europe up to this point:

1. as a fiction, a compelling simulation of "real life";
2. as the site of "Romance";
3. as a "nursery of letters" (Strether, the cultural child, the slow learner, metaphorically beginning to understand how to decipher the obscure "writing" of the metropolis and its inhabitants at the hands of this teachers, Maria Gostrey, Chad Newsome, Little Billham, and Mme. de Vionnet); and
4. as, by turns, a Grecian or Romantic landscape both distant and immanent.

His thoughts then turn to the small picture by Emilé Lambinet that he almost bought in his youth, a "particular production that had made him for the moment overstep the modesty of nature." Recalling the pastoral image (perhaps similar to the one below) calling upon the viewer to recollect nature even if, for Strether, the desire to possess it represents an overstepping of nature's boundaries, he then steps into his memory palace in a vain attempt "to assist at the restoration to nature of the whole far-away hour" spent at the shop of a Boston art-dealer, and the equally vain effort to "reconcile" this oddly-pigmented "special-green vision" in a "maroon-colored sanctum" with what he anticipates as a plunge into nature's modesties once he descends from the train.

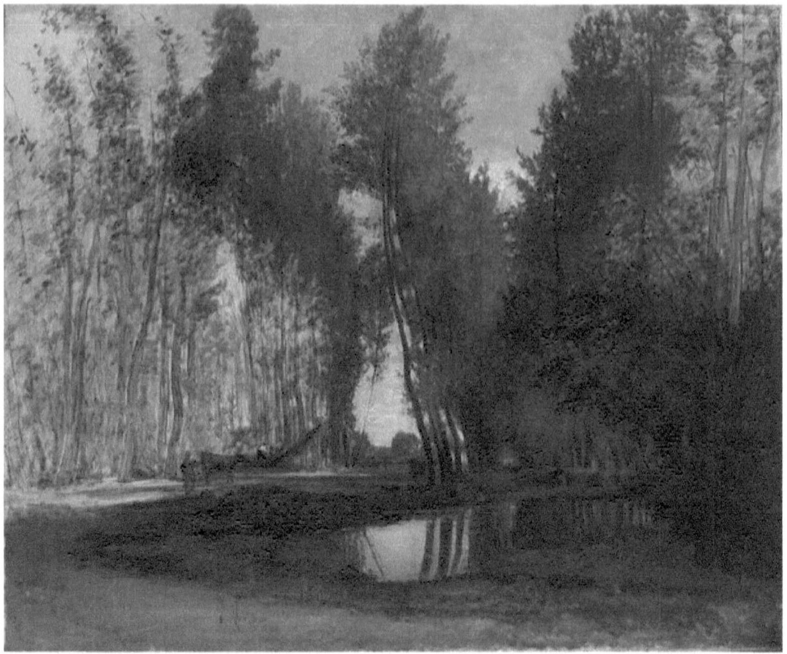

Figure 5.3. Émile Lambinet, *Clearing in a Beautiful Oak Forest*, c. 1845.

For Strether, in other words, experience is a matter of generating narrative frames around it, which may not to seem an especially illuminating precept in a novel written by Henry James, for whom, as we have seen, the only way to experience the unfolding scene of reality is through an elaborate narrative architecture. Yet the metanarrational overreach of this passage is remarkable, too visible, overdone. The recollection of the attempt to possess an artifice of nature in a memory wrought in terms of its own painterly contours as a preface to an encounter with nature in the theater of reality that James constructs for Strether suggests that James is foregrounding something other than the irony inherent in the notion that experience, as registered, reflected, and remembered, is always a fiction about or within a fiction. It also prefigures the hard truth about to be imposed upon Strether, as he relaxes after dinner in the picturesque inn with a view of the river, in the sighting of "a boat advancing round the bend and containing a man who held the paddles and a lady, at the stern, with a pink parasol."[15] The recognition of Chad's and Mme. de Vionnet's adulterous relationship—his blind encounter with the "real"—seemingly must, itself, be framed as experience converted into that which "had been wanted in the picture, had been wanted more or less all day, and had now drifted into sight, with the slow current, on purpose to fill up the measure."[16] It appears that Strether's raw recognition of the deceit underlying the picture of life constructed for him by his cultural mentors does not so much puncture that picture as complete it, the gap or black hole of the lie, once exposed, bringing to abrupt completion for all practical purposes the European journey of the dithering protagonist.

In essence, this scene of revelation and betrayal, with its *matryoshka*-doll effect of a figure within a figure within a figure, offers a paradoxical and highly reflexive view of the "total" experience of the "thing" or truth as only complete when the absence at its core is illuminated, the blankness of its immediacy recollected as a series of duplicative images that reveal their duplicity. The experience of the reality underlying all of the facades and gestures and language games of *The Ambassadors*—the form that recognition takes for Strether—occurs as the rude intrusion of the overwhelming quanta of the unknown into the pastoral totality, the flash of insight that only causes blindness. What transpires epistemologically in a novel by Henry James is registered "retinally" in a film by Alfred Hitchcock. Like Strether, Jefferies gets an eye-full (or several eyes-full) as he visually roams across the landscape of the apartment building, and the film implies, at least initially, that from his privileged, technologically enhanced perspective, he sees everything. For Miran Božovič, *Rear Window* is about the "lust of the eye" when one considers that the film is totally given over to gazing through eyes and windows that function as eyes. Jefferies's rear window, looking out upon Thorwald's rear window, reveals to the film's audience the "look" of the voyeur as he sits in a darkened room functioning as "a *camera obscura*—what unfolds in the room on this side of the window is precisely the inverted image of what unfolds beyond the window of the flat on the opposite side of the courtyard."[17] In turn, as Božovič suggests, the film reflexively looks back at us looking through the films multiple lenses—camera, window, retina: "As spectators, we are placed behind the retina of the giant eye viewing the images that appear on it."[18] But our role as spectators, just as Jefferies's role of voyeur/detective, is only activated when we notice what Božovič terms the "blot" in the image, for example, the singular instance of Jefferies observing Thorwald sitting in the dark with a lit cigar: like the red light on an operating surveillance camera, the bright orange light emitted by Thorwald's cigar is a kind of retinal afterimage signifying that he is "on," an eye for an eye, a gaze returned to the gazer, almost as a guarantee of his existence and purpose.

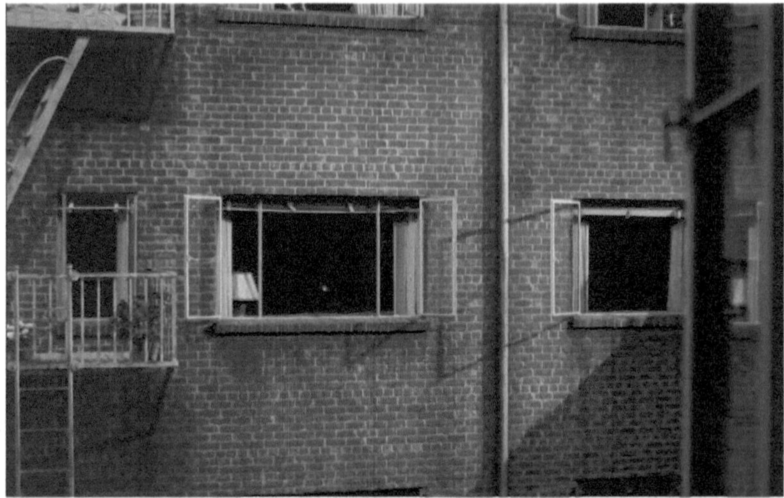

Figure 5.4. Thorwald's "eye." *Rear Window*, Paramount Pictures, 1954. Frame capture courtesy of Joshua Yumibe

Just as James stages *The Ambassadors* as a series of framed "scenes" that implicitly bear reference to the architecture of the novel while explicitly thematizing the relation between knowledge and perception as a matter of framing a reality, so Hitchcock in *Rear Window* visualizes the mechanics of filmmaking and the limitations of the technology that enables it as a primary aspect of its thematic content. As George Toles has commented, for all the focus on voyeurism and the gaze in *Rear Window*, what many considerations of the film only barely acknowledge "is its double existence as a conventional murder mystery . . . and as a commentary on the process of viewing and making a film."[19] I would reframe this formulation slightly, and extend it to *The Ambassadors,* in suggesting that both novel and film do not so much share a double existence as they do a single existence doubled, as both reflect on the capacity of the medium to draw a frame around a reality that exists as such by virtue of a blank spot. For James, the picture only makes sense when what has not been seen comes into view, an eventuality that destroys both frame and picture (and thus, in moralistic terms, the destruction of the perceiver's innocence; in epistemological terms, the destruction of the illusion of total knowledge; in psychoanalytic terms, the destruction of the myth of the unrepressed; etc.). For Hitchcock, the film's most revelatory moments come in a blinding camera bulb flash or a spot of light (a spotlight and a "blotlight") emerging out of nothingness, as if the very means by which life, truth, or being is registered in cinema exists at the same time as the ultimate obscuration of what can be seen. Rather than viewing these antimonies in James and Hitchcock only as signs of the "meta" in their work, or modernist acknowledgments of how much the materiality of the medium affects the content of the message, we can enlarge our perspective on the "aboutness" that merges *techne*, theme, and hermeneutic process in *The Ambassadors* and *Rear Window* by considering the ways in which they register *event*—seeing a couple in a boat sailing down the river, or blinding a murderer with a flashbulb. How does the actuality and immediacy of event affect what can be seen and not seen, framed and unframed in Hitchcock and James?

❧

The occurrences in *The Ambassadors* and *Rear Window* I have mentioned—Strether's sighting of Chad Newsome and Mme. de Vionnet on the river, Jefferies's temporary escape from a marauding Thorwald by means of popping flashbulbs, Jefferies's apprehension of Thorwald's sinister gaze communicated by the glow of a phallic, lit cigar (clearly, an especially threatening apparition given Jefferies's own impotence)—have in common their existence as particular forms of an event. Alain Badiou regards "event" as primarily a destabilizing of the "natural" order of the non-event that generates radical indeterminacy: "given that the essence of the event is to be undecidable with regard to its belonging to [a] situation, an event whose content is the eventness of the event . . . cannot, in turn, have any *form* than that of indecision. . . . The only representable figure of the concept of the event is the staging of its undecidability."[20] For Badiou, all events are singularities situated on the edge of what he terms the "void," or the place of non-being before being, but here he is referring to a specific form of the event generated by his consideration of Mallarmé's reflections on chance. It is precisely the suddenness, immediacy, and chanciness of the events I have cited in *The Ambassadors* and *Rear Window* that signifies their implicit commentary on what happens when "happens" is registered as something out of the blue, utterly indeterminate in the nanosecond of awareness. These are events "whose content is the eventness of the event"; indeed, this is Marcher's concern throughout

"The Beast in the Jungle," for he spends his sad life attempting to parse "eventness" in the absence of an event, only recognizing at the very end that what was to have happened to him, as the only man on Earth for whom nothing has happened, has already occurred, and it is that "nothing" that is the occurrence.

Parallel to the metanarrational and metacinematic tendencies of James's novel and Hitchcock's film, the key events upon which I have focused offer commentary on "eventness": their content, as events, is both ontological and epistemological; they signify their status as certain kinds of events as they register the modes of perception that have brought them about. They share these qualities and consequences:

1. They stage the indeterminate. Who is the subject of the gaze as Jefferies views Thorwald in the dark? What ambiguities of identification between Thorwald and Jefferies are created in the flash of light that blinds them both? For Strether, what narrative of events can any longer be trusted in a reality that, he learns, is constituted of partial, agenda-bound (that is to say, ideological) narratives?

2. They intrude upon fantasies of the natural, the normal, and the whole; their unexpectedness generates catastrophes in the primary sense of the word as a sudden overturning, or reversal of what is expected. Paradoxically, they disrupt and temporalize their own illusory immediacy. The interruption of Strether's idyll and the comic scrambling for explanatory narratives so that everyone can pretend they have not seen what they patently have seen is matched, visually, in *Rear Window*, as Jefferies, recognizing Thorwald's cigar-gaze upon him, suddenly moves back into his own darkness, as if that gesture could erase having been seen. These narrative and gestural reversals are vain attempts to undo the event and to return to the illusory normality of the unseen non-event (the pastoral setting; the darkness), but this is to return to the nothingness that was always there, behind and before the singularity of the event emerged as such.

3. They offer commentary, as "catastrophes," on the inverse relationship between experience and event writ large. They suggest, scriptively and visually, that the event exists as such

> only in recollections or reactions that are an aftereffect of the event itself. Contradictorily, they represent experience preceding event as the catalyst of its becoming-event and subsequently "remembered" corporeally (in gesture and physical reaction) and cognitively (in memory). This inverse dynamic and the contradiction upon which it rests echoes the "all-seeing blindness" I mentioned earlier that signifies full immersion into the present tense of the event in its immediacy: Strether's flash of insight in seeing the boat emerge behind the bank of a river; the flash of light that blinds and binds both Thorwald and Jefferies. The irony that both James and Hitchcock build into these representations and visualizations is that the event cannot be said to have been experienced in its purity and immediacy: in effect, they can neither be properly filmed or written, but only represented elliptically, their witnessing a matter of reaction and recollection occurring, temporally, as a displacement of the present into the immediate future or the distant past. Perhaps this explains in part why James and Hitchcock are such perfectionists, their art (especially late James; especially the Hitchcock of *Rear Window*, *Vertigo*, *The Birds*, and *Psycho*) so mannered, as they struggle to get it all and get it right.

These reflections on the connections to be made between the "meta" and the experiential compel a more detailed consideration of how events are experienced in James and Hitchcock cognitively and corporally. Here, I turn to Robert Nozick's political philosophy and the notable concept of the "experience machine" he developed in *Anarchy, State, and Utopia*. At the beginning of his reflection on individual experience within the state apparatus, Nozick asks, "What matters other than how people's experiences feel 'from the inside'?"[21] The question emerges from Nozick's discussion of individual human rights (in comparison to animal rights) and his libertarian goal of discerning the ways a minimalist state can protect those rights. The thought experiment of an "experience machine" exists in tandem to Nozick's revision of the Kantian conception of human rights, and represents his attempt to put human desire, or the pursuit of pleasure, in its proper place in the food chain of a moral code that protects the individual existing within the state apparatus. Nozick imagines this sci-fi scenario:

> Suppose there were an experience machine that would give you any experience you desired. Superduper neuropsychologists could stimulate your brain so that you would think and feel you were writing a great novel, or making a friend, or reading an interesting book. All the time you would be floating in a tank, with electrodes attached to your brain. Should you plug into this machine for life, preprogramming your life's experiences? If you are worried about missing out on desirable experiences, we can suppose that business enterprises have researched thoroughly the lives of many others. You can pick and choose from their library or smorgasbord of experiences . . . [and] while you're in the tank, you won't know you're there; you'll think it's all actually happening.[22]

Nozick goes on to explore the reasons for *not* plugging into the experience machine: beyond experience, there is action (we want to do certain things; we want to produce specific visible effects upon the world) and being (as he puts it, "the experience machine does not involve our desire to *be* a certain way").[23] While he doesn't fully address the questions that arise when we consider what matters other than experience, Nozick's thought experiment allows us to press the question of the relation between experience and event in James and Hitchcock that both consider as concomitant thematic and material concerns.

In *The Ambassadors*, Strether gives the young artist, "Little" Bilham, what is, perhaps, the most famous piece of advice in the James canon: "Live all you can; it's a mistake not to. It doesn't so much matter what you do in particular, so long as you have your life. If you haven't had that what have you had?"[24] This avuncular sentiment—a middle-aged reflection on how many opportunities for new experiences have been missed in youth—takes place at a garden party at the artist Gloriani's house in Paris, a contradictorily natural/artistic micro-world foreshadowing the pastoral micro-world Strether will enter that serves as the backdrop for another recognition illuminating the extent to which he has been deceived about the people and events ("life") he has encountered in France. In separating "living" from doing and suggesting the latter is irrelevant in its particulars ("it doesn't so much matter what you do") Strether is, in effect, counseling Bilham to plug into life conceived as a kind of experience machine, where the most important thing is to consume as many experiences as possible while you're young without regard to agency: how one acts, what one does, and what forms of interpellation (one's attachment to the social order while one is "experiencing") ensue. Nozick's account of the severe limitations of this model—it takes no account of act or purpose in relation to history or event—are in accord with the ironies James exposes in Strether's perspective as it is revealed in epiphanies taking place in these settings infused with the nature of artifice and the artifice of nature. In Gloriani's garden, Strether's advice is contextualized by the ever-present sense of belatedness that accompanies all of his recognitions: "There were some things that had to come in time if they were to come at all. If they didn't come in time they were lost for ever. It was the general sense of them that had overwhelmed him with its long slow rush."[25] On the one hand, Strether is counseling Bilham to "live all he can"—that is, to experience everything—in the instantaneous present of the experience machine. On the other, he appears to understand that experience can only become experience, just as event can only become event, in retrospect, the present continuously evaporating before the onset of a past that offers the opportunity for reflection. Outside of Strether, the floating consciousness of the novel's narrator appears to comprehend the double-bind inherent in Strether's thought: a desire for something ("life") that can only be registered experientially as a narrative of life, and thus a matter of a sufficiency of time, or enough time passing so that the story can take shape as inducing a set of relations between past and future. In a different context, this double-bind is on display in the French countryside, when Strether's moment of total immersion in the "all" of life that "France" has to offer is disrupted by the recognition of Chad and Mme. de Vionnet's affair, a counter-narrative with a secreted past that underscores the frailty of Strether's advice to Bilham when he is confronted with a life experience that shatters his complacency.

In *Rear Window*, Hitchcock's optics and Jefferies's voyeurism, facilitated by his paralysis, posit a conundrum as physical inaction ("doing") catalyzes a form of visual agency (a roving eye) that takes in "everything": here, experience is deferred, secondhand, and distanced. Jefferies's is technologically plugged into the experience machine of the courtyard, but everything that actually happens in the film—sex and murder, violence and desire in action—occurs elsewhere, in another apartment, across the gap between parallel structures. Even when he is about to experience violence firsthand as Thorwald bursts through his apartment door, Jefferies is saved by the spatial gap and temporal delay induced by the camera's flashbulbs, still an evolving technological innovation in 1954 that allowed for flash and aperture to be increasingly synchronized.[26] *Rear Window* is consistently—almost oppressively—insistent on its status as a form of visual machinery, its audience plugged into the same materially mediated spectacle as Jefferies experiences delivered through the lens of a 35mm camera that is "watching" other eyes and cameras watch each other. Yet the fact that the illusory immediacy of experience per se necessarily occurs visually and narratively in the form of a delay, across a gap, or in the body of another seen through a window or a camera lens renders the experience machine of *Rear Window* perverse in its secondhandedness. The function of Nozick's experience machine is to simulate whatever reality the user wishes, unmediated—the machinery disguising itself sufficiently to allow the user to experience the simulation as real—and in the present tense. But experience in both *Rear Window* and *The Ambassadors* is beset with delay and rupture, the medium through which the experience is registered foregrounded rather than disguised, the mediatory capacities of the medium serving as a critical framework for highlighting the temporal and spatial situatedness of the event to which experience is connected. The notion of "life" lived to the fullest in the present and experienced in full, as a totality, is exposed by James and Hitchcock as an illusion in their illusion-making machines.

Ever get lost in a novel so much that you lose track of time? Ever wander out of the darkened space of the movie theater startled and saddened at the daylight reality brutally intruding upon the cinematic reality in which you have been fully immersed for two hours? However much James and Hitchcock might want the reader/viewer to experience their work in this fashion, the actualities of *The Ambassadors* and *Rear Window* militate against this: one might say their authorial/directorial impulses are in some form of contestation with their impulses as sheer entertainers. Or, one might say, alternatively, that the contestation of these impulses is hardwired into their art, and further, that the novel and film as forms of mediation necessarily contain (or fail to contain) these oppositional energies as their *raison d'être*.

In *The Ambassadors*, the epiphanic moment of immersion/illumination that Strether experiences in a Paris suburb doubles back upon itself in disenchantment that takes place a mere hour or so later when he sees Chad and Mme. de Vionnet together. The temporal delay that occurs between the two instances separates, in effect, the repetition of an event experienced *in* time; that is, what Strether experiences, and what James registers metafictionally, is precisely a catastrophe, a turn of events that fatally links immersion and recognition, or in other terms, experience and consciousness. Unlike the thought experiment of the experience machine, where consciousness *is* experience, for James, the two are only one in the sense that the former emerges as the consequence of the time it takes for the latter to occur, rendering life "unnatural." In the experience machine, there is no temporality, no reflexivity, just sheer experience rendered transparently as a simulated (and, in reality, impossible) "natural" totality; in James, an artist who works in a medium whose very materials are time and space, there is nothing but time and the disenchantments it entails.

Given that in *Rear Window* the medium in question is film, for which the notion of illumination has a material analogue in the projection of light through space onto a screen, there are distinct intermedial similarities to the representation of experience that occurs in James. As we have seen, the film's optics and its thematic investments in voyeurism necessarily depend upon a series of temporal and spatial delays and relays between the actuality of event and the experience of occurrence. These delays/relays generate both hermeneutic questions (what are we actually seeing? what is the meaning of what we are seeing? why are we seeing this now?) and technical questions (how is what we are seeing affected by the lens or device through which we are seeing it? how is the technology either getting in the way of, or facilitating what has occurred or what is about to occur?). With great deliberation, Hitchcock plants these questions within the genre of a "whodunit," or more precisely, a film that asks if who done it really did it. This emphasis on the veracity of seeing and experience parallels James's emphasis on the temporal delay between enchantment and demystification in *The Ambassadors*. Strether is propelled out of the experience machine (the simulation of "nature" in the suburban forest) and into a brutal encounter with the "reality" that has been operating behind the scenes all of the time in the course of the novel. But, of course, since experience is necessarily partial, limited, and framed in all of James, this recognition is a matter of cognitive and perceptual time-lapses that derail immediacy (analogous to the technological mediations of *Rear Window*) and generate indeterminacy. Both James and Hitchcock, narratively and cinematically, reflect upon the fatality of experience as a matter of time, its accidental nature spelled out in recognitions of what has already occurred, whether it be "epiphany" or murder, event itself registered as a form of uncertainty that entails only further questions about the nature of what one has experienced. Almost the entirety of *Rear Window* is given over to skepticism about what the voyeuristic eye really sees; much of *The Ambassadors*—ultimately a comic and very funny novel, as *Rear Window* is a comic and very funny film—seems devoted to watching others pull the wool over Strether's eyes and watching him cooperate in pulling the wool over his own. Experience machines they are not.

Epilogue

A Brief Reflection on *Melancholia*

Lars von Trier's *Melancholia* (2011) is a film that imagines the end of everything that we know and see. Envisioning the collision of Planet Earth with a rogue planet, it portends the end of both the human and the planetary, thus framing and exploding the (now) fabled Anthropocene by obliterating what comes after. The film's ending sequence portrays a woman, her sister, and her child huddling beneath a makeshift structure that mocks the fragility of the sacred sanctuary while the all-consuming aftershock of interstellar collision overtakes and consumes everything. The final shots precede both the collapse of a totality (the cinematic totality of the film as well as the totality of the Earth as a planetary singularity) and the negation of a future that can no longer be thought or visualized beyond the instantaneous present of catastrophe.

Like much of James's late fiction, *Melancholia* is about a future that can only be conceived as a blank space, an after/math to reality that exposes the extent to which aesthetics and "world" are fabricated on the basis of an evacuated totality, one full of holes. Yet it is a totality of uneven, microscopic surfaces and elevations raised by specificity, illuminated by vision, gesturing toward its own status as artistic medium. Like Tarantino's *Kill Bill* films, *Melancholia* is a pastiche of cinematic reference, as if von Trier wanted to get it all in before the ending of this film that portends the ending of all filming. Bergman's slow-paced, slightly off-kilter domestic sequences inform the wedding scenes in the first part of *Melancholia*; Kubrick's pastoral longueurs, particularly those of *Barry Lyndon*, are reflected in scenes such as that where Justine, played by Kirsten Dunst, lies naked on a riverbank, slowly coming back to life

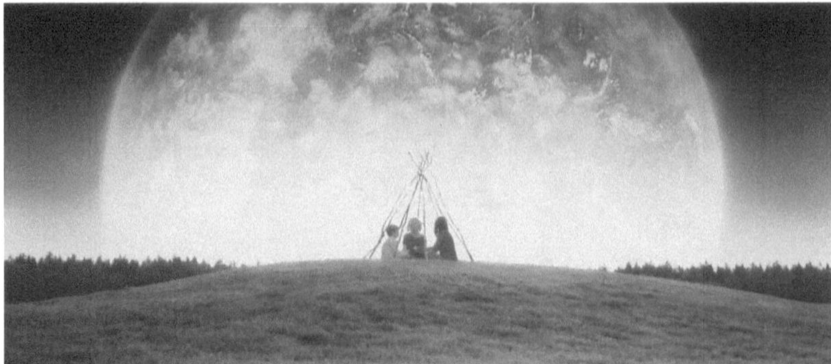

Figure E.1. The end of the world in *Melancholia. Melancholia*, Nordisk Film, 2011. Frame capture courtesy of Joshua Yumibe.

from a spell of catatonic depression as the planet dies; traces of Woody Allen's slapstick (especially in Part One), Tarkovsky's *Solaris* (1972), and von Trier's own *Antichrist* (2009) can be found throughout the film. This is not even to begin to elaborate upon the elaborate network of references, especially in Part One, to modern painting and design, or to the history of art across the film, interestingly captured in the video essay "Little Museum of Horrors: The Artistic References of Lars von Trier."[1] *Melancholia* is thus a metacinematic film about life-threatening depression, where von Trier visually and narratively studies the equation between depression, the end(s) of cinema, and the end of the world that adds up to a future that can only be enlivened and "known" as the rehearsal of a lost past. Brief images of the marriage that might have been, blown up on the wedding day itself, the happiness that might have come, had depression not intervened, that life that might have been, had a stray planet not come into contact with Planet Earth—these flash across the doomed backdrop of the film as it moves steadily towards a catastrophe that can only be fully imagined after the credits being to roll.

In his classic essay on affect and mortality, "Mourning and Melancholia," Freud distinguishes between the work of mourning and melancholy: in the former, detachment from the dead person or lost object is achieved through the "work"; in the latter, the work of mourning has failed because this detachment has not occurred—instead, the inability to "let go" has resulted in persistent condition of loss and dread. In melancholy, there is no end point because, as Eric Savoy argues in his queer reading of melancholy in James's "The Jolly Corner" (1908), "according to Freud, melancholia, which arises from the trauma of loss [that] cannot be resolved in the work of ordinary mourning, results in a splitting of the ego" in which "the ego establishes an identification with the lost object . . . In Freudian theory, melancholia arises from the subject's ambivalent and unresolved relation with the lost object."[2] I have considered the ways that "The Beast in the Jungle" anticipates an individual future bound over to a past of lost opportunities, objects, and persons (May Bartram, in particular) that can only be recognized as such when Marcher is standing over May's grave, attempting too late to perform the work of mourning, not just for the lost other, but also the lost self. To this degree, "The Beast in the Jungle" can be identified as a melancholic narrative that temporalizes melancholy by portraying its origins, as it were, in a future that appears (to Marcher, at least) as fated as it is indeterminate. Savoy, pursuing a line of inquiry opened by Eve Kosofsky Sedgwick, would explain this trajectory as one that occurs when the "other" is one's own closeted sexuality, yet we might explain it in other terms one that occurs when the self (any self) recognizes that the future, short-term or long-term, is equally certain and uncertain: the certainty pertaining to the assuredness of self-extinction at some point, the uncertainty generally pertaining to the temporal and circumstantial details. *Melancholia* extends this temporal trajectory to a cosmic (or at least a planetary) level: we know that, at some point, the planet Earth will no longer exist, that it is just a matter of astronomical time. But to the extent that *we* identify with the planet, the imagined loss of that object parallels and portends the collective demise of the collective "human," an extinction that we know we are hastening as each day passes, and as the future recedes into the lost opportunities of the past. The film, then, may be characterized as attempting to perform the work of mourning over the lost object of the planet and the lost objects of humanity—a work that it can never complete cinematically since it can only imagine, allegorically, what this loss might actually be, and fret over it.

In "The Beast in the Jungle," Marcher, too, can only imagine the ultimacy of the future in the form of an allegory—that of the imaginary beast that will spring upon him out of the jungle, initiating an event that will be both terrifying and sublime in its suddenness and surprise. More deeply than James's protagonist ever can, the reader recognizes that the content of the event is nothing, and that the story is in part an allegory about the non-event of an end (to the story, to writing) that cannot be registered, but only anticipated. The language of Marcher's final moment in the story as he stands over May Bartram's grave is overwrought with anticipation about what is still to come: "He saw the Jungle of his life and saw the lurking Beast; then, while he looked, perceived it, as by a stir of the air, rise, huge and hideous, for the leap that was to settle him. His eyes darkened—it was close; and, instinctively turning, in his hallucination, to avoid it, he flung himself, face down, on the tomb."[3] The resemblances between this final sentence of James's story and the final scenes of von Trier's film are remarkable, almost as if the writer and the filmmaker were impossibly having a conversation about how to represent and visualize "the end." The same gesture of avoidance (Marcher, "turning, in his hallucination, to avoid it"; Claire, flinching in the second before the advancing cloud of destruction overtakes them) can be seen in both, registering the autonomic flinch that occurs in the face of mortality, individual or global. This story and film about the end must end, of course, but in doing so, both appear to incorporate an instinctual evasion—a noticeable disavowal—of what might come after. Narratively, both story and film have been promising, as it were, to represent that aftermath. In *Melancholia*, Claire's husband, John, stands for the hope for a future as he obsessively scans the skies through a homemade device for a near-miss of planetary collision; in "The Beast in the Jungle," James clearly stages the encounters between Marcher and May as a series of near misses in which it might dawn on Marcher that what he is looking for in the opacity of the future is sitting right in front of him—at least this is one of the possible readings of the story.

But near misses are not of interest to either James or von Trier, nor is a nearly failed heterosexual romance (one that offers a screen for closeted sexuality), nor a dystopic/domestic version of "when worlds collide" that didn't at the last minute. Rather, both are invested in imagining an end that cannot be imagined, and representing both the attempt and the failure to do so. The future, in this reading, is collapsed into a form of the instantaneous present—the nanosecond before the catastrophic cloud blows humanity away; the instant just preceding Marcher's leap into the abyss of the grave. Both James and von Trier project what this future looks like (visually and rhetorically)—a projection that exists at the very limits of their chosen medium's capacity to complete its trajectory. As we have seen in Lukács's and Bazin's foundational work on the novel and film, the aesthetics of singularity and partiality engaged by James and the filmmakers I consider here is at odds with some totality—whether the "human scene," the end of the world, or a panoptic social order—

that appears to lurk behind a novelistic or cinematic recapitulation of a world. It is a condition of modernity to be torn by this contradiction that necessitates a reflection on the limitation of one's art at the same time one is making it.

James is not the only modern novelist to have recognized this paradox, but he certainly is the first to so fully integrate it into his work. Hitchcock, Tarantino, Haneke, Nolan, and von Trier are not the only filmmakers to have recognized it either, but they are chief among those cinematic auteurs mid-century to twenty-first century to have established visual "reflexivity" as central to the content and materiality of the medium, and the medium itself as a cracked mirror that limns what can be envisioned. At the same time their work, like James's late fictions, is empowered by the angles and specificities that view the world as fractal and partial, replete with odd singularities, distracting trajectories, and incomplete pictures. For some, the condition of modernity that accords with an aesthetics of partiality and singularity is calamitous, as it appears to comply with an anti-collective politics; for others, it is liberating, in that it appears to resist the impulse toward totalities and totalitarianism that a vision of "the whole" entails. The contradiction lies everywhere and elsewhere: that it persists in the fictions and films considered here is a tribute to their capacity to question and expose the innate conceptions of knowing and seeing upon which their work depends.

Notes

Introduction

1. Henry James, preface to *The Ambassadors* in *The Art of the Novel: Critical Prefaces*, ed. R. P. Blackmur (New York: Scribner's, 1962), 311.

2. Tom Gunning, "To Scan a Ghost: The Ontology of Mediated Vision," *Grey Room* 26 (2007): 97, 98.

3. Miram Hansen, "The Mass Production of the Senses: Classical Cinema as Vernacular Modernism," *Modernism/modernity* 6, no. 2 (1999): 60.

4. Susan M. Griffin and Alan Nadel, "Reading James with Hitchcock, Seeing Hitchcock Through James," in *The Men Who Knew Too Much: Henry James and Alfred Hitchcock*, ed. Susan M. Griffin and Alan Nadel (New York: Oxford University Press, 2012), 14.

5. These and numerous other facts related to the history of the film industry year by year can be found on the AMC "Film History Milestones" pages at https://www.filmsite.org/milestones.html.

6. Susan M. Griffin, "Henry James and Film," in *A Companion to Henry James*, ed. Gregory W. Zacharias (New York: Wiley-Blackwell, 2008), 472–89. While I do not pursue James's relation to film through theories of adaptation here, Griffin's work in this area is significant and certainly influential for any consideration of James and film; see Susan M. Griffin, *Henry James Goes to the Movies* (Lexington, KY: University of Kentucky Press, 2002). Griffin's earlier book, *The Historical Eye: The Texture of the Visual in Late James* (Boston, MA: Northeastern University Press, 1991), has also been influential for my discussion of visuality, James, and cinema. While Griffin deploys a markedly different critical framework in focusing on the history of the psychology of perception to understand how James's protagonists "think" visually, her conceptualization of James's "narrative strategies" that are "intimately tied" to the ways in which characters experience "visual perception [as] a process that takes place in and over time" reflecting "the temporal nature of their identities" deeply informs my own understanding of James's cinematic imagination (4).

7. Fredric Jameson, *Signatures of the Visible* (New York: Routledge, 1990), 1.

8. Jameson, *Signatures*, 8.

9. Henry James, preface to *The Portrait of a Lady* in *Art of the Novel*, 45–46.

10. The earliest instances that the OED cites for the use of the word "cinematic" as relating to filmmaking or the aesthetics of cinematography occur in 1912 and 1913, the latter in—of all places—William Dean Howells's travelogue, *Familiar Spanish Travels*, where a changing landscape is captured in the phrase "the wheat stubble now disappeared with cinematic suddenness." Despite the coincidence of James's friend and mentor's making early use of a word arising from the relatively new medium of film, it is unlikely that James would have been familiar with it or thought it an appropriate descriptor for his narrative practice.

11. Mark Seltzer, *Henry James and the Art of Power* (Ithaca NY: Cornell University Press, 1984), 40, 153. For an informative discussion and critique of Seltzer's reflections on James, see Janet Gobler-Hover, "The Critical Deconstruction of Henry James," *Texas Studies in Literature and Language* 29, no. 2 (1987): 215–35.

12. Gobler-Hover summarizes Seltzer's argument as one that highlights the "essential dishonesty and evasiveness in James's aesthetics, but . . . accepts this dishonesty nonjudgmentally as a necessary correlative to the exercise of power" ("Critical Deconstruction," 217). This "dishonesty" is embodied in James appearing to allow a form of free will and consciousness in his characters (fomenting the illusion that they are able to think what they want and act as they will despite social norms) while, in fact, exercising authorial power in the creation of this illusion as such—a "problem" that is inherent in the genre of the novel writ large. While I am not in disagreement with Seltzer's view, I am more interested in the ways in which the aesthetics inferred in the "house of fiction" analogy reveal a split in James's perspective between the partial and the total that informs his cinematic approach to narrative considered further on.

13. For a discussion of James indebtedness to Balzacian realism, see William W. Stowe, *Balzac, James, and the Realistic Novel* (Princeton, NJ: Princeton University Press, 2014).

14. Sheila Teahan, *The Rhetorical Logic of Henry James* (Baton Rouge, LA: Louisiana State University Press, 1995), 2. In her meticulous analysis of James's figural logic, Teahan goes on to describe a paradox in his aesthetics somewhat different from the one I will shortly introduce in a comparison of "the house of fiction" analogy to Bazin's notion of total cinema. For Teahan, a contradiction or countercurrent rests in James's installation of a central consciousness or reflector in a protagonist only to, in effect, destroy it: "a recurring feature of the Jamesian reflector is a self-dismantling or self-negation that is staged at some point. . . . This dismantling takes the form of the destruction or effacement of the central consciousness itself, which is to say the character who embodies that consciousness, through a death or sacrifice enacted at the

level of plot or figuration" (3). This "self-dismantling," Teahan suggests, reflects James's awareness of the extent to which any representations of "consciousness" have no foundation in any available representational schema, even as he writes novels that claim to represent consciousness operating through descriptions of thought and character. See also Ross Labrie's inventory of James's various figural and literal descriptions of consciousness across his novels and prefaces: "Henry James's Idea of Consciousness," *American Literature* 39, no. 4 (1968): 517–29.

15. Henry James, preface to *Roderick Hudson*, in *The Art of the Novel: Critical Prefaces*, ed. R. P. Blackmur (New York: Scribner's, 1934), 4. It is no accident, in my view, that James chooses the figure of an ocean or sea to represent the "human scene" he speaks of in the Preface to *The Portrait of a Lady*, where the focus is on "seeing" and the relationship between what is known and what is seen. This is but one of many examples of metafictional punning of the kind Lynda Zwinger discusses throughout *Telling in Henry James: The Web of Experience and the Forms of Reality* (New York: Bloomsbury, 2015).

16. James, preface to *Roderick Hudson*, 4, 5.

17. James, preface to *Roderick Hudson*, 5.

18. James, preface to *Roderick Hudson*, 5–6.

19. In her reading of the "house of fiction" analogy, Alice Gavin considers the ways in which James "dispositions" the artist in relation to the scene being viewed, so that nothing is viewed directly, but only known, like an aberration of starlight, at an angle. She turns to early film as well to see how "dispositioning" is an intermedial trait, locating James "less as an intermediary between realism and realism after realism, than the anxiety of mediation itself." See Alice Gavin, *Literature and Film, Dispositioned: Thought, Location, World* (New York: Palgrave Macmillan, 2014), 65.

20. György Lukács, *Theory of the Novel: An Historico-Philosophical Essay on the Forms of Great Epic Literature*, trans. Anna Bostock (Cambridge, MA: MIT Press, 1974), 49.

21. Lukács, *Theory of the Novel*, 56.

22. Lukács, *Theory of the Novel*, 60.

23. Clearly, James's "cinematic imagination" has its roots in what Bazin regards as the anticipatory medium of film, photography; in this regard, following Bazin, the "idea" of cinema may have come to James in some fashion via his knowledge of photography. There are several discussions of James's interest in photography and how it may have influenced his fiction, and of his relationship with A. L. Coburn, who shot James's portrait as well as the frontispieces for each volume of the New York Edition. I do not pursue the explicit connections between James and photography here as I am not focusing on questions of influence, authorial or intermedial, but of particular interest is Edward L. Schwarzschild, "Revising Vulnerability: Henry James's Confrontation with Photography," *Texas Studies in Language and Literature* 38, no. 1 (1996): 51–78; Miroslawa Bucholtz,

"Real, Surreal, Hyperreal: Photography and the Novel According to Henry James, André Breton, and W. G. Sebald," in Miroslawa Bucholtz and Grzegorz Koneczniak, eds., *The Visual and the Verbal in Film, Drama, Literature and Biography* (New York: Peter Lang, 2012), 151–86; Ralph F. Bogardus, *Pictures and Texts: Henry James, A. L. Coburn, and New Ways of Seeing in Literary Culture* (Ann Arbor, MI: UMI Research Press, 1984); and Julie Grossman, " 'It's the Real Thing': Henry James, Photography, and the Golden Bowl," *Henry James Review* 15, no. 3 (1994): 309–28.

24. André Bazin, *What Is Cinema?*, trans. Hugh Gray, 2nd ed. (Berkeley, CA: University of California Press, 2004), 19, 20.

25. Bazin, *What Is Cinema?*, 21.

26. While I do not take up Jay David Bolter's and Richard Grusin's notion of "remediation" in this book as they are focused on the history of visual representations, the concept is relevant to a discussion to any intermedial claims that can be ascribed to the modern novel and film as a modern genre in suggesting that "new" media inevitably reinscribe older media through double logics of "transparency" and "hypermediacy." It is this latter that is most applicable to the anxiety produced as James, Lukács, and Bazin confront both the desire and the impossibility of replicating a totality, for "hypermediacy" (for Bolter and Grusin, a logic hard-wired into the materiality of a medium, even print, as such) which "acknowledges multiple acts of representation and makes them visible" and "offers a heterogeneous space, in which representation is conceived of not as a window onto the world, but rather as 'windowed' itself—with windows that open on to other representations or other media." This "acknowledgement" of a potential for infinite regress in the act of representation conceived in strikingly similar visual terms is implicit in James's "house of fiction" analogy—one that both powers his aesthetic and reveals the limitations of the novelist's aspirations to manufacture a world out of whole cloth. See Jay David Bolter and Richard Grusin, *Remediation: Understanding New Media* (Cambridge, MA: MIT Press, 1999), 33–34.

27. While it is not entirely clear at what point James began to be referred to as "the master," the title of one of James's stories, "The Lesson of the Master" (1888), as well as frequent references to "master" and "mastery" in the prefaces, the title the final volume of Leon Edel's five-volume biography of James, *The Master, 1901–1916*, and even something as recent as Colm Tóibín's fictionalization of James in late life in *The Master* (2004) contribute to this labelling of James as an *auteur* supreme.

28. Fredric Jameson, *Postmodernism or, the Cultural Logic of Late Capitalism* (Durham, NC: Duke University Press, 1991), 272.

29. William Faulkner, *As I Lay Dying* (New York: Vintage, 1964), 261.

30. See Murray Pomerance, "Nothing Sacred: Modernity and Performance in *Catch Me If You Can*," in *Cinema and Modernity*, ed. Murray Pomerance (New Brunswick, NJ: Rutgers University Press, 2006), 211–33.

31. Slavoj Žižek, *The Parallax View* (Cambridge, MA: MIT Press, 2006), 17.

32. An interesting version of this reversal is posed by the logician Raymond Smullyan, in *The Chess Mysteries of Sherlock Holmes*: "So Watson,' continued Holmes with a chuckle, " 'is it not amusing how it sometimes happens that to know the past, one must first know the future?' " Raymond Smullyan, *The Chess Mysteries of Sherlock Holmes: 50 Tantalizing Problems of Chess Detection* (Mineola, NY: Dover, 1979), 52.

33. The phrase is used by Barth in an essay that speaks to the continuance of the novel as a form struggling through Cold War apocalypticism and theoretical movements that declared the author (and, in some ways, the genre) to be dead. See John Barth, "The Literature of Exhaustion," in *The Friday Book: Essays and Other Non-Fiction* (Baltimore: Johns Hopkins University Press, 1984), 62–76.

Chapter 1

1. Herbert N. Schneidau, *Sacred Discontent: The Bible and Western Tradition* (Berkeley: University of California Press, 1977), particularly ch. 1, 1–49.

2. Hugh Kenner, *The Pound Era* (Berkeley: University of California Press, 1971), 4.

3. For an excellent discussion of Hitchcock's modernism, see David Trotter, "Hitchcock's Modernism," *Modernist Cultures* 5, no. 1 (2010): 106–26.

4. James, preface to *Roderick Hudson*, 5.

5. James, preface to *Roderick Hudson*, 3–4.

6. Tom Cohen, *Anti-Mimesis: From Plato to Hitchcock* (New York: Cambridge University Press, 1994), 237.

7. James, preface to *Roderick Hudson*, 5–6.

8. On James's fetishization of objects, which can be viewed as the embodiment of "the lure of detail," see Bill Brown, "A Thing About Things: The Art of Decoration in the Work of Henry James," *Henry James Review* 23 (2002): 222–32.

9. Slavoj Žižek, *The Ticklish Subject: The Absent Centre of Political Ontology* (London: Verso, 1999), 304.

10. D. A. Miller, *Hidden Hitchcock* (Chicago: University of Chicago Press, 2016), 17–18.

11. Henry James, "In the Cage," in *Henry James: Selected Tales*, ed. John Lyon (New York: Penguin, 2001), 314.

12. James, "Cage," 316. As far as I can determine, the protagonist of "In the Cage" remains anonymous throughout.

13. Mark Goble, "Wired Love: Pleasure at a Distance in Henry James and Others," *ELH* 74, no. 2 (2007): 398.

14. James, "Cage," 318.

15. James, "Cage," 328. This will not be the last time we will see the word "silver" associated with the word "clue" in James's fiction; see chapter 3.

16. James, "Cage," 324.

17. James, "Cage," 370.

18. James, "Cage," 330.

19. Henry James, "The Figure in the Carpet," in *Henry James: Selected Tales*, 291.

20. James, "Cage," 323.

21. James, "Cage," 323.

22. James, "Cage," 327, 325.

23. James, "Cage," 369.

24. Eric Savoy, "The Jamesian Thing," *Henry James Review* 22, no. 3 (2001): 274.

25. James, "Cage," 371.

26. James, "Cage," 369, 370.

27. This information gleaned from "A Short History of Telephone Numbers" on the Art.Lebdev website at https://www.artlebedev.com/mandership/91/.

28. John Carlos Rowe, *The Other Henry James* (Durham, NC: Duke University Press, 1998), 161. Rowe's chapter on "In the Cage" focuses on the relationship between technology and gender in the figure of the story's telegrapher-protagonist, and James's anxiety, revealed in this encoding, about loss of authorial control over "information" as such.

29. Žižek, *Ticklish Subject*, 158.

30. For a comprehensive and lively discussion of the technical difficulties Hitchcock encountered in making the film, see Tony Lee Moral, *The Making of Hitchcock's* The Birds (Harpenden, UK: Kamera Books, 2013).

31. There are numerous discussions of Hitchcock and the Cold War, the most comprehensively economic, perhaps, being Thomas M. Leitch, "It's the Cold War, Stupid: An Obvious History of the Political Hitchcock," *Literature/Film Quarterly* 27, no. 1 (1999): 3–15. But see also the fascinating pseudo-documentary *Double Take* (2010), directed by Johan Grimonprez and scripted by novelist Tom McCarthy that projects Alfred Hitchcock meeting his double and serves as an allegory for the deadly reciprocity that existed between the USSR and the USA during the Cold War and that came to a head in the Cuban Missile Crisis.

32. Hitchcock's treatment of Hedren in similar fashion is widely contended; see Donald Spoto, *The Dark Side of Genius: The Life of Alfred Hitchcock* (Boston: Little, Brown, 1983) as well as Hedren's account of their relationship in *Tippi: A Memoir* (New York: William Morrow, 2016), where she recalls that Hitchcock sexually assaulted her during the film of *The Birds* and *Marnie*.

33. The theoretical framework I am deploying is clearly Lacanian/Žižekian, to which I offer only glancing reference rather than full explication here as that is beyond my purposes. But see Žižek's foundational commentary on Hitchcock in

Looking Awry: An Introduction to Jacques Lacan through Popular Culture (Boston: MIT Press, 1991), 67–106, as well as Christopher D. Morris, "Reading the Birds and *The Birds*," *Literature/Film Quarterly* 28, no. 4 (2000): 250–58.

34. Henri Lefebvre, *Introduction to Modernity* (London: Verso, 1995), 21.

Chapter 2

1. Harry Harootunian, "The Benjamin Effect: Modernism, Repetition, and the Path to Different Cultural Imaginaries," in *Walter Benjamin and the Demands of History*, ed. Michael P. Steinberg (Ithaca NY: Cornell University Press, 1996), 77.

2. Giorgio Agamben, *Infancy and History: Essays on the Destruction of Experience*, trans. Liz Heron (New York: Verso, 1993), 96.

3. Agamben, *Infancy*, 16.

4. Agamben, *Infancy*, 16.

5. Henry James, *What Maisie Knew* (New York: Penguin, 2010; orig. 1897), 5.

6. James, *Maisie*, 18.

7. The most complete reading of the work of catachresis in James is Sheila Teahan's compelling *The Rhetorical Logic of Henry James* (Baton Rouge: Louisiana State University Press, 1995).

8. See Kevin Ohi, *Innocence and Rapture: The Erotic Child in Pater, Wilde, James, and Nabokov* (New York: Palgrave Macmillan, 2005), for a key discussion of childhood, eroticism, and aestheticism in "The Turn of the Screw" that considers the figure of the child via queer theory. This discussion paves the way for Ohi's book-length discussion in *Henry James and the Queerness of Style* (Minneapolis, MN: University of Minnesota Press, 2011), which engages questions of belatedness observable stylistically and thematically in James's late fiction that contrasts and conjoins with my understanding of temporality in *Maisie* experience occurring before (it's) time.

9. Mary Anne Doane, *The Emergence of Cinematic Time* (Cambridge, MA: Harvard University Press, 2002), 19, 170.

10. *Kill Bill: Vol. 2*, directed by Quentin Tarantino (Miramax, 2004); this is my transcription of the film dialogue, which differs at various points (sometimes considerably) from the shooting script, available at https://www.imsdb.com/scripts/Kill-Bill-Volume-1-&-2.html.

11. J. Hillis Miller, *Versions of Pygmalion* (Cambridge, MA: Harvard University Press, 1990), 41.

12. Rowe, *Other Henry James*, 153.

13. Henry James, preface to *What Maisie Knew* in *Art of the Novel*, 142.

14. Henry James, *Maisie*: 4.

15. James, preface to *What Maisie Knew*, 140.

16. Sharon Cameron, *Thinking in Henry James* (Chicago: University of Chicago Press, 1989), 64.

17. Cameron, *Thinking*, 65.

18. Cameron, *Thinking*, 65.

19. James, *Maisie*, 23.

20. James, *Maisie*, 84.

21. James, *Maisie*, 156.

22. James, *Maisie*, 206.

23. James, *Maisie*, 220.

24. James, *Maisie*, 256.

25. James, *Maisie*, 4.

26. James, *Maisie*, 210.

27. James, *Maisie*, 211.

28. James, *Maisie*, 211.

29. James, *Maisie*, 80–81.

30. James, *Maisie*, 206.

Chapter 3

1. Žižek, *Parallax View*, 17.

2. James, preface to *The Portrait of a Lady* in *Art of the Novel*, 46.

3. James, preface to *The Portrait of a Lady*, 46.

4. *Caché*, dir. Michal Haneke (Les films des losange, 2005).

5. R. P. Blackmur, introduction to James, *Art of the Novel*, vii.

6. Tom, "To Scan a Ghost," 97, 98.

7. Immanuel Kant, *The Critique of Judgement*, 2nd ed., rev. trans. J. H. Bernard (London: Macmillan, 1914), §69. Available at http://ebooks.adelaide.edu.au/k/kant/immanuel/k16ju.

8. William James, *Psychology: The Briefer Course* (Mineola, NY: Dover Publications, 2001; orig. 1892), 20.

9. James, *Maisie*, 206.

10. For a somewhat different reading of James's anxieties about the novels contradictions that emphasizes its moral and rhetorical antinomies, see Sheila Teahan, "*What Maisie Knew* and the Improper Third Person," *Studies in American Fiction*, 21, no. 2 (1993): 127–40.

11. James, preface to *Roderick Hudson*, 5–6.

12. Žižek, *Parallax View*, 125.

13. Žižek, *Parallax View*, 135.

14. Rebecca Walkowitz, "Ishiguro's Floating Worlds," *ELH*, 68, no. 4 (2001): 1049.

15. James, preface to *The Golden Bowl* in *Art of the Novel*, 345.

16. James, preface to *Golden Bowl*, 340.

17. See also Lynda Zwinger's brilliant discussion of fish and "silver clues" in *Telling in Henry James*, 67–84.

18. Jameson, *Postmodernism*, 9.

19. For a compelling discussion of how *Caché* conveys that which cannot be seen—the repressed content of Western history—see Murdoch Jennings, "Žižek's Dialectics: Critique of Ideology and Emancipatory Politics in Michael Haneke's *Caché* (2005)," *International Journal of Žižek Studies*, 8, no. 2 (2014): 1–30.

20. Catherine Wheatley, "Secrets, Lies & Videotape," *Sight & Sound*, 16, no. 2 (2006): 34.

21. For another excellent discussion of the film to French colonial history in Algiers, see Ipek A. Celik, "'I Wanted You to Be Present': Guilt and the History of Violence in Michael Haneke's *Caché*," *Cinema Journal*, 50, no. 1 (2010): 59–80.

22. Maurice Blanchot, *The Writing of Disaster*, trans. Ann Smock (Lincoln: University of Nebraska Press, 1995), 137.

23. Žižek, *Looking Awry*, 143.

24. The familiar figure of Pierrot recurs across myriad genres, mediums, and national literatures since its inception in the seventeenth century. I find it quite interesting that Pierrot is an important figure in the avant-garde cinema that clearly influences Haneke's work; such films as Jean-Luc Godard's *Pierrot le Fou* (1965), Kenneth Anger's *Rabbit's Moon* (1972), and Ingmar Bergman's *In the Presence of a Clown* (1997) feature avatars of Pierrot. For more on Pierrot's influence on modernist and avant-garde art and film, see Martin Green and John Swan, *The Triumph of Pierrot: The Commedia dell'Arte and the Modern Imagination* (University Park, PA: Pennsylvania State University Press, 1986).

25. Paul Gilroy, *Postcolonial Melancholia* (New York: Columbia University Press, 2005), 98.

Chapter 4

1. Sylviane Agacinski, *Time Passing: Modernity and Nostalgia*, trans. Jody Gladding (New York: Columbia University Press, 2003), 12.

2. For a key discussion, see Paul Connerton, *How Modernity Forgets* (Cambridge, UK: Cambridge University Press, 2009).

3. Agacinski, *Time Passing*, 16.

4. Sigmund Freud, *The Psychopathology of Everyday Life*, trans. Alan Tyson (New York: W. W. Norton, 1965), 6.

5. James, "Beast in the Jungle," 431.

6. Agamben, *Infancy and History*, 100, 96–97.

7. Unfortunately, and ironically, this 2002 blog entry is no longer available on the internet, where "memories" such as this are erased in massive quantities minute by minute. I can assure the reader that I did not make it up, though perhaps, not too fancifully, in the collective "mind" of the internet, "we" did, but forgot about it.

8. Eric Savoy, "The Queer Subject of 'The Jolly Corner,'" *Henry James Review* 20, no. 1 (1999): 1–21. See also Nicholas Dames, who provides an insightful discussion of how James, "a guardian of his own memories of novelistic origin . . . is also continually presenting James-as-artist as a guardian of memory itself, as a force acting against the all too pervasive disappearances and erasures of everyday social life" ("The Disease of Temporality; or, Forgetful Reading in James and Lubbock," *Henry James Review* 25, no. 3 [2004]: 246–47). Dames shows how, for James, reading the novel is to engage in a temporal progression through form; from this perspective, Marcher would be, amongst other things, a bad reader who "skips" through time, as one might skip through the chapters of a novel, anxiously jumping ahead to a conclusion that never comes, and thus missing the "time" of the narrative, it's substance per se.

9. Patrick O'Donnell, *Latent Destinies: Cultural Paranoia in Contemporary U.S. Narrative* (Durham, NC: Duke University Press, 2000), especially pp. 24–43.

10. James, "Beast," 429.

11. James, "Beast," 459.

12. James, "Beast," 460.

13. Agamben, *Infancy and History*, 100.

14. Agamben, *Infancy and History*, 93.

15. James, "Beast," 459–60.

16. Jacques Derrida, *Spectres of Marx: The State of Debt, the Work of Mourning, and the New International*, trans. Peggy Kamuf (New York: Routledge, 1994), 70.

17. James, "Beast," 461.

18. James, "Beast," 432–33.

19. Jorge Luis Borges, *Ficciones* (New York: Grove Press, 1962), 114.

20. A now-defunct web resource, the health-cares.net website, provided this most straightforward and helpful definition of anterograde amnesia when I originally researched the topic, and I have not uncovered any documented resources since then that provide the same kind of economic definition for the layperson. But see also Oliver Sacks's moving case studies of short-term memory loss in *The Man Who Mistook His Wife for a Hat and Other Clinical Tales* (New York: Simon and Schuster, 1985), especially "The Lost Mariner" (23–42), which recounts the story of a man who remembers nothing that has happened to him after a decades-old trauma, and "A Matter of Identity" (108–15), the story of a man who "remembered nothing for more than a few seconds. He was continually disoriented. Abysses of amnesia continually opened beneath him, but he would

bridge them, nimbly, by fluent confabulations and fictions of all kinds" (109). Nolan's protagonist combines these two manifestations of memory loss: Leonard cannot remember anything after the head trauma from which he suffers (and the film leaves open the possibility that even this is a "nimble confabulation") so that, in time, this will become a long-term amnesia—a time that he "fills in" with the fictions and repetitions that form a minute-by-minute response to the ongoing loss of short-term memory.

21. Having reached its apogee in the last forty years of the twentieth century, Polaroid technology was in decline by the time *Memento* was made: with the advent of digital photography and the cell phone, Polaroid Corporation filed for bankruptcy in 2001, the year *Memento* was released.

22. See Richard Dawkins, *The Selfish Gene* (New York: Oxford University Press, 1989), especially pp. 189–202.

23. For a revealing discussion of this nexus, see Noël Carroll, "*Memento* and the Phenomenology of Comprehending Motion Picture Narration" in *Memento*, edited by Andrew Kania (New York: Routledge, 2009), 127–46.

24. Christopher Nolan, "Memento: A Screenplay by Christopher Nolan, final draft August 10, 1999," http://www.nolanfans.com/library/pdf/memento-screenplay.pdf, scene 13.

25. Nolan, "Memento," scene 24.

26. Doane, *Emergence of Cinematic Time*, 140.

27. Nolan, "Memento," scene 21.

28. Nolan, "Memento," scene 58.

Chapter 5

1. Henry James, *The Ambassadors* (New York: Penguin, 1981), 281.

2. Many versions of this picturesque totality exist in James, from early to late, but perhaps nowhere is the picturesque "whole," which depends upon a kind of allegorical typology, so thoroughly and rapidly punctured as it is in this scene from *The Ambassadors*. An early version of this (for James) comic trope occurs in "A Passionate Pilgrim" (1871), where the narrative "we" finds, in the vision of the village green of an English village lost in the past, a negation of absence: "Passing out upon the highroad, we came to the common browsing-patch, the 'village green' of the tales of our youth. Nothing was absent: the shaggy, mouse-colored donkey, nosing the turf with his mild and huge proboscis, the geese, the old woman—THE old woman, in person, with her red cloak and her black bonnet, frilled about the face and double-frilled beside her decent placid cheeks—the towering ploughman with his white smock-frock puckered on chest and back, his sort corduroys, his mighty calves, his big rural face. We greeted these things as children greet the loved pictures of a storybook lost and mourned

and found again. We recognized them as one recognizes the handwriting on letter-backs" (Henry James, "A Passionate Pilgrim," in *The Novels and Tales of Henry James,* Volume XIII [New York: Macmillan, 1909], 364). Note that here, as in *The Ambassadors,* the scene is converted into a readable text.

3. See Sharon Cameron's description of how "consciousness," for James, can appear as omniscient: "consciousness [i]s all-pervasive . . . Disparate points of view are not significant because the exemplify conflicts of consciousness. Rather, they are significant because they exemplify the omnipresence of consciousness, identifying it with all points of view, even in those in opposition, demonstrating thereby that there is no place in the book where consciousness has not been made to penetrate" (*Thinking in Henry James,* 5). Cameron is discussing implicit notions of consciousness in James's *The American Scene,* and while this is an eloquent summary of the notion, for James, in its most idealized form, it is also one often disputed in late James, where proclamations of omniscience (the "penetration" of consciousness everywhere) often precede a fall into a recognition of the severe limitations of one's vision.

4. Zwinger, *Telling in Henry James,* 9.

5. James, *Ambassadors,* 281. See Eric Haralson, *Henry James and Queer Modernity* (Cambridge, UK: Cambridge University Press, 2003), especially pp. 102–33, for a compelling discussion of the frequent use of the word "queer" in the novel, especially as it applies to Strether's affective life and the representation of his masculinity.

6. Throughout, my rendering of the complicitous epistemological relationship between blindness and insight is informed by de Man's "The Rhetoric of Blindness: Jacques Derrida's Reading of Rousseau," in which he asserts that the critical insights of the reader are gained through a contradictory processes of envisioning and formulation: "insight seems . . . to have been gained through a negative moment that animates the critics thought, an unstated principle that leads his language away from the asserted stand, perverting and dissolving his stated commitment to the point where it becomes emptied of substance, as if the very possibility of assertion had been put into question. Yet it is this negative, apparently destructive labor that led to what could legitimately be called insight" (Paul de Man, *Blindness and Insight: Essays on the Rhetoric of Contemporary Criticism,* 2nd ed. rev. [Minneapolis: University of Minnesota Press, 1983], 103).

7. James, *Ambassadors,* 301.

8. The classic reading of gender and sexuality in *Rear Window* upon which I rely here is that of Tania Modleski, "The Master's Dollhouse: *Rear Window,*" in her *The Women Who Knew Too Much: Hitchcock and Feminist Theory,* 2nd ed. (New York: Routledge, 2005), 69–88.

9. Tom Cohen, *Hitchcock's Cryptonomies, Vol. 1: Secret Agents* (Minneapolis: University of Minnesota Press, 2005), 67–68.

10. See Laura Mulvey, "Visual Pleasure and Narrative Cinema," *Screen* 16, no. 3 (1975): 6–18, for what remains one of the most foundational discussions of the entangled relationship between camera, image, and audience in film.

11. A number of James's critics note the ways in which James theatricalizes identity, particularly in his early fiction, but I would suggest this tendency continues into the late fiction, particularly with James's failed dramatic experiments of the 1890s—a time when he was obsessed with theatrical impulses. For an array of interesting perspectives on the theatricalization of identity in James across his career, see Victoria Coulson, *Henry James, Women and Realism* (Cambridge, UK: Cambridge University Press, 2007), 60–96; Sara Blair, "Realism, Culture, and the Place of the Literary: Henry James and *The Bostonians*," in *The Cambridge Companion to Henry James*, edited Jonathan Freedman (Cambridge, UK: Cambridge University Press, 1998), 151–68; and Haralson, *Henry James and Queer Modernity*.

12. James, *Ambassadors*, 281, 7, 25, 84, 178.

13. James, *Ambassadors*, 278.

14. James, *Ambassadors*, 278.

15. James, *Ambassadors*, 283.

16. James, *Ambassadors*, 283.

17. Miran Božovič, "The Man Behind His Own Retina," in *Everything You Always Wanted to Know about Lacan (But Were Afraid to Ask Hitchcock)*, edited by Slavoj Žižek (New York: Verso, 1992), 161–62.

18. Božovič, "Man Behind His Own Retina," 162.

19. George E. Toles, "Alfred Hitchcock's *Rear Window* as Critical Allegory," *boundary* 2, no. 16 (1989): 235. As he works through the film's "optics of suspicion" (226), Toles provides Marxist, deconstructionist, and feminist readings of the film in which he juxtaposes his own reading that attempts, as I do here, to merge Hitchcock's metacinematic tendencies with the interpretable content of the film because, as for James, the *techne* of the novel is embedded in its thematics, so for Hitchcock, the *techne* of the film is one with its voyeuristic dramatization of male voyeurism, or its "locating and defining . . . the hole or gap that desperation has carved out of the center of this bourgeois idyll" (228–29), or its "commentary on the threatened or degraded status of immediate events" (229). I will be returning to this third conceptualization shortly in discussing Badiou's conception of event in the film; Toles's essay remains one of the fundamental readings of *Rear Window* as a film that critiques its own making.

20. Alain Badiou, *Being and Event*, trans. Oliver Feltham (London: Continuum, 2005), 193–94.

21. Robert Nozick, *Anarchy, State, and Utopia* (New York: Basic Books, 1974), 42.

22. Nozick, *Anarchy, State, and Utopia*, 42–43. There have, of course, been numerous commentaries comparing Nozick's thought experiment to films like

The Matrix and *Total Recall*, as well as the emergence of "total" virtual worlds in computer gaming open world simulations and MMOs (massively multiplayer online games). In many of these, Nozick's conception of the experience machine is seen as a cautionary tale about the danger of privileging the heightened experiences of virtual worlds over experience in the sociopolitical order, which is fraught with the complexities to be sorted out when individual desire is in conflict with individual rights and the collective apparatus of the state. For a discussion of the connections to be made between Nozick, film (particularly in regard to Bazin's "The Myth of Total Cinema"), and gaming virtual realities, see Stefano Gualeni, "The Experience Machine: Existential Reflections on Virtual Worlds," *Journal of Virtual Worlds Research* 9, no. 3 (2016): 1–10.

23. Nozick, *Anarchy, State, and Utopia*, 44.

24. James, *Ambassadors*, 110.

25. James, *Ambassadors*, 110.

26. What had been a technology only available to professional photographers up until World War II, the flash bulb was mass-marketed following the war as devices either attached to or built into inexpensive cameras for the general public; Jefferies, however, appears to be using more professional gear in the film. See Kate Flint's *Flash: Photography, Writing, and Surprising Illumination* (New York: Oxford University Press, 2018), especially chapter 4, "Stopping Time," 77–99, for a fascinating discussion of the history of flash photography as it registers modernist concerns with temporality and spatiality.

Epilogue

1. See Titouan Ropert, "Little Museum of Horrors: The Artistic References of Lars von Trier," July 20, 2017, available at https://filmschoolrejects.com/little-museum-horrors-artistic-references-lars-von-trier/. Though the essay is confined to references to painting, it makes clear the extent to which von Trier's films make use of citation to the arts in general—film, painting, music, and design.

2. Savoy, "Queer Subject of 'The Jolly Corner,'" 12.

3. James, "Beast in the Jungle," 461.

Bibliography

Agacinski, Sylviane. *Time Passing: Modernity and Nostalgia*. Translated by Jody Gladding. New York: Columbia University Press, 2003.

Agamben, Giorgio. *Infancy and History: Essays on the Destruction of Experience*. Translated by Liz Heron. New York: Verso, 1993.

AMC. *Film History Milestones*. Accessed June 11, 2020. www.filmsite.org/milestones.html.

Badiou, Alain. *Being and Event*. Translated by Oliver Feltham. New York: Continuum, 2005.

Barth, John. *The Friday Book: Essays and Other Non-Fiction*. Baltimore, MD: Johns Hopkins University Press, 1984.

Bazin, André. *What is Cinema?* Translated by Hugh Gray. 2nd. Berkeley: University of California Press, 2004.

Blair, Sara. "Realism, Culture, and the Place of the Literary: Henry James and the Bostonians." In *The Cambridge Companion to Henry James*, edited by Jonathan Freedman, 151–68. New York: Cambridge University Press, 1998.

Blanchot, Maurice. *The Writing of Disaster*. Translated by Ann Smock. Lincoln: University of Nebraska Press, 1995.

Bogardus, Ralph F. *Pictures and Texts: Henry James, A. L. Coburn, and New Ways of Seeing in Literary Culture*. Ann Arbor MI: UMI Research Press, 1984.

Bolter, Jay David, and Richard Grusin. Grusin, J. David Bolter and Richard. *Remediation: Understanding New Media*. Cambridge, MA: MIT Press, 1999.

Borges, Jorge Luis. *Ficciones*. New York: Grove Press, 1962.

Božovič, Miran. "The Man Behind His Own Retina." In *Everything You Always Wanted to Know about Lacan (But Were Afraid to Ask Hitchcock)*, edited by Slavoj Žižek, 161–62. New York: Verso, 1992.

Brown, Bill. "A Thing About Things: The Art of Decoration in the Work of Henry James." *Henry James Review* 23 (2002): 222–32.

Bucholtz, Miroslawa. "Real, Surreal, Hyperreal: Photography and the Novel According to Henry James, André Breton, and W. G. Sebald." In *The Visual and the Verbal in Film, Drama, Literature and Biography*, edited by Miroslawa Bucholtz and Grzegorz Koneczniak, 151–86. New York: Peter Lang, 2012.

Cameron, Sharon. *Thinking in Henry James*. Chicago: University of Chicago Press, 1989.

Carroll, Noël. "*Memento* and the Phenomenology of Comprehending Motion Picture Narration." In *Memento*, edited by Andrew Kania, 127–46. New York: Routledge, 2009.

Celik, Ipek A. " 'I Want You to Be Present': Guilt and the History of Violence in Michael Haneke's Cache." *Cinema Journal* 50.1 (2010): 59–80.

Cohen, Tom. *Anti-Mimesis: From Plato to Hitchcock*. New York: Cambridge University Press, 1994.

———. *Hitchcock's Cryptomies, Vol. 1: Secret Agents*. Minneapolis MN: University of Minnesota Press, 2005.

Connerton, Paul. *How Modernity Forgets*. Cambridge: Cambridge University Press, 2009.

Coulson, Victoria. *Henry James, Women and Realism*. New York: Cambridge University Press, 2007.

Dames, Nicholas. "The Disease of Temporality; or, Forgetful Reading in James and Lubbock." *Henry James Review* 25.3 (2004): 246–53.

Dawkins, Richard. *The Selfish Gene*. New York: Oxford University Press, 1989.

Derrida, Jacques. *Spectres of Marx: The State of Debt, the Work of Mourning, and the New International*. Translated by Peggy Kamuf. New York: Routledge, 1994.

Doane, Mary Anne. *The Emergence of Cinematic Time*. Cambridge, MA: Harvard University Press, 2002.

Edel, Leon. *Henry James*. 5 Volumes. Philadelphia: J. B. Lippincott, 1962.

Faulkner, William. *As I Lay Dying*. New York: Vintage, 1964.

Flint, Kate. *Flash: Photography, Writing, and Surprising Illumination*. New York: Oxford University Press, 2018.

Freud, Sigmund. "Mourning and Melancholia." In *The Standard Edition of the Complete Psychological Works of Sigmund Freud, Volume XIV (1914–1916): On the History of the Psycho-Analytic Movement, Papers on Metapsychology and Other Works*, edited by James Strachey, 237–58. New York: Vintage, 1998. First published 1917.

Freud, Sigmund. *The Psychopathology of Everyday Life*. Translated by Alan Tyson. New York: W. W. Norton, 1965.

Gavin, Alice. *Literature and Film, Dispositioned: Thought, Location, World*. New York: Palgrave Macmillan, 2014.

Gilroy, Paul. *Postcolonial Melancholia*. New York: Columbia University Press, 2005.

Goble, Mark. "Wired Love: Pleasure at a Distance in Henry James and Others." *ELH* 74.2 (2007): 397–427.

Gobler-Hover, Janet. "The Critical Deconstruction of Henry James." *Texas Studies in Literature and Language* 29.2 (1987): 215–35.

Green, Martin, and John Swan. *The Triumph of Pierrot: The Commedia dell'Arte and the Modern Imagination*. University Park: Pennsylvania State University Press, 1986.

Griffin, Susan M., and Alan Nadel. "Reading James with Hitchcock, Seeing Hitchcock Through James." In *The Men Who Knew Too Much: Henry James and Alfred Hitchcock*, edited by Susan M. Griffin and Alan Nadel, 3–29. New York: Oxford University Press, 2012.

Griffin, Susan M. "Henry James and Film." *A Companion to Henry James*, edited by Gregory W. Zacharias, 472–89. New York: Wiley-Blackwell, 2008.

———. *Henry James Goes to the Movies*. Lexington: University of Kentucky Press, 2002.

———. *The Historical Eye: The Texture of the Visual in Late James*. Boston: Northeastern University Press, 1991.

Grimonprez, Johan, dir. *Double Take*. Brussels, Belgium: Zap-O-Matik, 2009.

Grossman, Julie. "'It's the Real Thing': Henry James, Photography, and the Golden Bowl." *Henry James Review* 15.3 (1994): 309–28.

Gualeni, Stefano. "The Experience Machine: Existential Reflections on Virtual Worlds." *Journal of Virtual World Research* 9.3 (2016): 1–10.

Gunning, Tom. "To Scan a Ghost: The Ontology of Mediated Vision." *Grey Room* 26 (2007): 94–127.

Haneke, Michael, dir. *Caché*. Paris, France: Les films des losange, 2005.

———. *Funny Games*. Paris, France: Concorde, 1997.

———. *The White Ribbon*. Vienna, Austria: Filmladen, 2009.

Hansen, Miriam. "The Mass Production of the Senses: Classical Cinema as Vernacular Modernism." *Modernism/modernity* 6.2 (1999): 59–77.

Haralson, Eric. *Henry James and Queer Modernity*. Cambridge: Cambridge University Press, 2003.

Harootunian, Harry. "The Benjamin Effect: Modernism, Repetition, and the Path to Different Cultural Imaginaries." In *Walter Benjamin and the Demands of Hisory*, edited by Michael P. Steinberg, 62–87. Ithaca NY: Cornell University Press, 1996.

Hedren, Tippi. *Tippi: A Memoir*. New York: William Morrow, 2016.

Hitchcock, Alfred, dir. *The Birds*. Universal City, CA: Universal Pictures, 1963.

———. *The Man Who Knew Too Much*. London, UK: Gaumont-British Picture Corporation, 1934.

———. *Marnie*. Universal City, CA: Universal Pictures, 1964.

———. *Psycho*. Hollywood, CA: Paramount Pictures, 1960.

———. *Rear Window*. Hollywood, CA: Parmount Pictures, 1954.

———. *Vertigo*. Hollywood, CA: Paramount Pictures, 1958.

James, Henry. *The Ambassadors*. New York: Penguin, 1981.

———. *The Art of the Novel: Critical Prefaces*. Edited by R. P. Blackmur. New York: Scribners, 1962.

———. "The Beast in the Jungle." In *Henry James: Selected Tales*, edited by John Lyons, 426–61. New York: Penguin, 2001.

———. "The Figure in the Carpet." In *Henry James: Selected Tales*, edited by John Lyons, 284–313. New York: Penguin, 2001.

———. *The Golden Bowl*. New York: Penguin, 2009.

———. "In the Cage." In *Henry James: Selected Tales*, edited by John Lyon, 314–84. New York: Penguin, 2001.

———. "The Lesson of the Master." In *Henry James: Selected Tales*, edited by John Lyon, 118–67. New York: Penguin, 2001.

———. "A Passionate Pilgrim." In *The Novels and Tales of Henry James Vol. XIII*, 335–434. New York Edition. New York: Macmillan, 1909.

———. "The Turn of the Screw." In *Henry James: Complete Stories 1892–1898*, 635–740. New York: Library of America, 1996.

———. *What Maisie Knew*. New York: Penguin, 2010.

———. *The Wings of the Dove*. New York: Penguin, 2008.

James, William. *Psychology: The Briefer Course*. Minneola, NY: Dover, 2001. First published 1892.

Jameson, Fredric. *Postmodernism, or the Cultural Logic of Late Capitalism*. Durham, NC: Duke University Press, 1992.

———. *Signatures of the Visible*. New York: Routledge, 1990.

Jennings, Murdoch. "Žižek's Dialectics: Critique of Ideology and Emancipatory Politics in Michael Haneke's Cache." *International Journal of Žižek Studies* 8.2 (2014): 1–30.

Kant, Immanuel. *The Critique of Judgement*. Edited by J. H. Bernard. Translated by J. H. Bernard. 2nd ed. London: Macmillan, 1914.

Kenner, Hugh. *The Pound Era*. Berkeley: University of California Press, 1971.

Labrie, Ross. "Henry James's Idea of Consciousness." *American Literature* 39.4 (1968): 517–29.

Lebedev, Artemy. "A Short History of Telephone Numbers." June 18, 2002. https://www.artlebedev.com/mandership/91.

Lefebvre, Henri. *Introduction to Modernity*. London: Verso, 1995.

Leitch, Thomas M. "It's the Cold War, Stupid: An Obvious History of the Political Hitchcock." *Literature/Film Quarterly* 27.1 (1999): 3–15.

Lukács, György. *Theory of the Novel: An Historical-Philosophical Essay on the Forms of Great Epic Literature*. Translated by Anna Bostock. Cambridge, MA: MIT Press, 1974.

Man, Paul de. *Blindness and Insight: Essays on the Rhetoric of Contemporary Criticism*. 2nd ed. Minneapolis: University of Minnesota Press, 1983.

Miller, D. A. *The Hidden Hitchcock*. Chicago: University of Chicago Press, 2016.

Miller, J. Hillis. *Versions of Pygmalion*. Cambridge, MA: Harvard University Press, 1990.

Modleski, Tania. *The Women Who Knew Too Much: Hitchock and Feminist Theory*. 2nd ed. New York: Routledge, 2005.

Moral, Tony Lee. *The Making of Alfred Hitchcock's* The Birds. Harpenden, UK: Kamera Books, 2013.

Morris, Christoper D. "Readings the Birds and The Birds." *Literature/Film Quarterly* 28.4 (2000): 250–58.

Mulvey, Laura. "Visual Pleasure and Narrative Cinema." *Screen* 16.3 (1975): 6–18.

Nolan, Christopher, dir. *Memento*. Los Angeles, CA: Newmarket, 2000.

———. "Memento: A Screenplay by Christopher Nolan." Script. Final Draft August 10, 1999. http://www.nolanfans.com/library/pdf/memento-screenplay.pdf.

Nozick, Robert. *Anarchy, State, and Utopia*. New York: Basic Books, 1974.

O'Donnell, Patrick. *Latent Destinies: Cultural Paranoia in Contemporary U.S. Fiction*. Durham, NC: Duke University Press, 2000.

Ohi, Kevin. *Henry James and the Queerness of Style*. Minneapolis: University of Minnesota Press, 2011.

———. *Innocence and Rapture: The Erotic Child in Pater, Wilde, James, and Nabokov*. New York: Palgrave Macmillan, 2005.

Pomerance, Murray. "Nothing Sacred: Modernity and Performance in Catch Me If You Can." In *Cinema and Modernity*, edited by Murray Pomerance, 211–33. New Brunswick, NJ: Rutgers University Press, 2006.

Ropert, Titouan. "Little Museum of Horrors: The Artistic References of Lars von Trier." July 20, 2017. https://filmschoolrejects.com/little-museum-horrors-artistic-references-lars-von-trier.

Rowe, John Carlos. *The Other Henry James*. Durham, NC: Duke University Press, 1998.

Sacks, Oliver. *The Man Who Mistook His Wife for a Hat and Other Clinical Tales*. New York: Simon and Schuster, 1985.

Savoy, Eric. "The Jamesian Thing." *Henry James Review* 22.3 (2001): 268–77.

———. "The Queer Subject of 'The Jolly Corner.'" *Henry James Review* 20.1 (1999): 1–21.

Schneidau, Herbert. *Sacred Discontent: The Bible and Western Tradition*. Berkeley: University of California Press, 1977.

Schwarzschild, Edward L. "Revising Vulnerability: Henry James's Confrontation with Photography." *Texas Studies in Literature and Language* 38.1 (1996): 51–78.

Seltzer, Mark. *Henry James and the Art of Power*. Ithaca, NY: Cornell University Press, 1984.

Smullyan, Raymond. *The Chess Mysteries of Sherlock Holmes: 50 Tantalizing Problems of Chess Detection*. Mineola, NY: Dover, 1979.

Spoto, Donald. *The Dark Side of Genius: The Life of Alfred Hitchcock*. Boston: Little, Brown, 1983.

Stowe, William W. *Balzac, James, and the Realistic Novel*. Princeton, NJ: Princeton University Press, 2014.

Tarantino, Quentin, dir. *Kill Bill: Vol. 1*. California: Miramax, 2003.

———, dir. *Kill Bill: Vol. 2*. California: Miramax, 2004.

———. "Kill Bill Volume 1 & 2." Script. *The Internet Movie Script Database*. Accessed June 11, 2020. https://www.imsdb.com/scripts/Kill-Bill-Volume-1-&-2.html.

Teahan, Sheila. *The Rhetorical Logic of Henry James*. Baton Rouge: Louisiana State University Press, 1995.

———. "What Maisie Knew and the Improper Third Person." *Studies in American Fiction* 21.2 (1993): 127–40.

Tóibín, Colm. *The Master*. New York: Scribner's, 2004.

Toles, George. "Alfred Hitchcock's Rear Window as Critical Allegory." *boundary 2*, no. 16 (1989): 225–45.

Trier, Lars von, dir. *Melancholia*. Copenhagen, Denmark: Nordisk Film, 2011.

Trotter, David. "Hitchcock's Modernism," *Modernist Cultures* 5, no. 1 (2010): 106–26.

Walkowitz, Rebecca. "Ishiguro's Floating World's." *ELH* 68.4 (2001): 1049–76.

Wheatley, Catherine. "Secrets, Lies & Videotape." *Sight & Sound* 16.2 (2006): 32–36.

Žižek, Slavoj. *Looking Awry: An Introduction to Jacques Lacan through Popular Culture*. Boston: MIT Press, 1991.

———. *The Parallax View*. Cambridge, MA: MIT Press, 2006.

———. *The Ticklish Subject: The Absent Centre of Political Ontology*. London: Verso, 1999.

Zwinger, Lynda. *Telling in Henry James: The Web of Experience and the Forms of Reality*. New York: Bloomsbury, 2015.

Index

www.ingramcontent.com/pod-product-compliance
Lightning Source LLC
LaVergne TN
LVHW090809070826
844660LV00022B/1127

* 9 7 8 1 4 3 8 4 8 2 7 6 7 *